WORSHIP THE WAY
IT WAS MEANT TO BE

Worship the Way It Was Meant to Be

15 Biblical Principles
for Knowing and Loving God

Bob Wetmore

CHRISTIAN PUBLICATIONS, INC.
CAMP HILL, PENNSYLVANIA

CHRISTIAN PUBLICATIONS, INC.
3825 Hartzdale Drive, Camp Hill, PA 17011
www.christianpublications.com

Faithful, biblical publishing since 1883

Worship the Way It Was Meant to Be
ISBN: 0-87509-971-8
© 2003 by Bob Wetmore
All rights reserved
Printed in the United States of America

03   04   05   06   07   5   4   3   2   1

*Note: Italicized words in Scripture quotations
are the emphasis of the author.*

CONTENTS

Introduction

My friend came home from his missionary tour recently. He had a heavy heart. He had preached in quite a few churches over a period of eight weeks, and almost all were—or at least had been—in turmoil. In every case, the churches were fighting over worship styles. It may seem ironic, but worship has probably divided more American churches in the past ten years than any other issue.

Writers have produced a myriad of books on worship. I am particularly interested in the books written to end worship wars. Some tell us that we can end the wars by accepting or rejecting contemporary music. Others want us to blend contemporary music with more traditional hymns. Some criticize all evangelical worship and urge churches to turn back to liturgies. Many books offer insights on how to worship or how to lead a church into biblical worship. I suppose the authors believe that if we only knew *how* to worship, we would not fight over it.

Some writers teach on the biblical doctrines of worship, hoping to redirect churches by reeducating them. That's good, but many base their views on what certain parts of the Old Testament teach about worship. To them, the New Testament *seems* to say very little about worship, so these authors turn to Isaiah 6 and the Psalms, for example, for what they teach.

A better approach exists. They could study the Bible the way Isaiah and David did, starting from the beginning, Genesis 1:1. Then they could arrive at worship principles step-by-step, the way God revealed them. That way, when they came to the Psalms, they would

understand worship with virtually the same foundations David brought to worship. Almost no one, however, has used this method—until now.

God revealed His will about worship in progressive
steps, and this book follows that progression. I began my
study of worship at the beginning—Genesis 1:1—and
ended it with the book of Revelation. I believe this is the
only way to find a proper understanding of what the Bible actually teaches on the subject. My approach is re-
flected in this book.

This book searches for biblical worship principles. It
does not cover every mention of worship in the Bible. Instead, I ask a series of questions about worship—the kind
of questions Christians either are or should be asking—and then give the biblical answers to those questions. Each principle builds upon the previous one.

I have written to help those who are struggling to re-
solve worship conflicts. I wish every Christian would read
this book, not just those in churches where worship is the
source of conflict, because it discusses some of the most
important truths one will encounter in the Christian life.
People who are in the midst of worship conflicts, however, really need to read this book. My approach to healing the division caused by worship wars is to deal with attitudes and thinking. Our actions must change. Therefore, our attitudes must change. That's why our thinking
must change. *Worship the Way It Was Meant to Be* is all
about changing our thinking and our attitudes so that
proper actions will follow.

To help you apply these worship principles to real life,
I will introduce you to Troy Smith, the new worship director at First Community Church of Gainesville,

Florida. A worship war is dividing his congregation, and Pastor Jeff, the senior pastor, is doing everything he can to bring healing. Even though this story is fictional, it reflects experiences I encountered as a pastor and church member. It also flows from the ministries and experiences of others.

This book has a central principle: The cross of Jesus Christ is at the heart of all worship. I am utterly convinced that Jesus Christ is the subject of the Bible. The Old Testament continually speaks of Him and prepares the way for His coming. And Jesus stands at the center of the New Testament. Take Jesus away from the Bible, and you have nothing but meaningless principles and useless history.

Take Jesus away from worship, and all you have is sentimental drivel. Yet fewer and fewer churches sing hymns and choruses that mention Him. The hymns and choruses they do sing seldom glory in His cross. The greatest hope I have for this book is that Christians will again realize that the cross is the center of all we are. Only then will we learn to worship the way it was meant to be.

ONE

Why Should I Worship God?

QUESTION:

Why should I worship God?

PRINCIPLE 1:

A: God created me so that I could know Him and love Him. Worship flows from my love relationship with God.

B: All relationships are based on trust. In my worship, I step out and trust what God has said about Himself and His ways.

C: When I sin, I am refusing to love God and therefore cannot worship Him. My sin also drives me to hide from Him.

Sunday morning service, February 4

Troy and Isabelle nervously opened the church door. Already church members were beginning to fill the pews. First Community Church of Gainesville, Florida, was getting ready for Sunday morning worship. Troy Smith braced himself to lead his first service as the new minister of worship.

When Pastor Jeff Daniels interviewed the Smiths, he warned them that the church was in turmoil. Pastor Rick, the last worship leader, had brought innovations in worship. A third of the congregation loved his style. Another third hated it. The board leaned against the new worship and asked Rick to leave. That decision left the church in shock. Rick's supporters wrestled with their anger. Some immediately abandoned the church. The rest were waiting to see how Troy and Isabelle might work to heal the wounds. Among the remaining church members, the traditionalists wanted to return to the hymnal. The contemporary worship people wanted to keep Rick's innovations. The rest just wanted peace.

And Troy? He wanted God's best for the church. He knew that choosing a particular worship style would not solve anything. This battle ultimately was not about music. It was about loving God. If the congregation did not learn that, it would not learn anything. Yet how could Troy make them understand?

Isabelle squeezed Troy's hand and silently prayed, *Lord, give Troy wisdom and give them love.*

* * *

Loving God Comes First

The members of First Community Church thought that they were trying to solve a worship problem. Actually, they were struggling with a priority problem.

What is, after all, life's first priority? To fulfill our purpose. And what is our purpose? To know God and to love Him. That's why He created us.

Isn't this what Jesus taught us?

> One of the teachers of the law . . . asked him, "Of all the commandments, which is the most important?"
>
> "The most important one," answered Jesus, "is this: 'Hear, O Israel, the Lord our God, the Lord is one. Love the Lord your God with all your heart and with all your soul and with all your mind and with all your strength' " (Mark 12:28-30).

Before members of First Community Church could deal with worship styles, they needed to learn to love God with all their heart, soul, mind and strength.

God created Adam and Eve in His image so that they could carry on a love relationship with Him and each other. The key to understanding anything we do is to understand how that love relationship should work. Relationships grow through communication. With Adam and Eve, God began the relational process by having a desire deep within His heart. That desire was His perfect will for humankind. He translated that desire into words and then spoke those words to Adam.

The next part of the process belonged to Adam. Adam had to hear God's words and actively work at considering them. What did God mean by His words? What did those words suggest that God wanted to see happening in Adam's heart or in his behavior? How did God want Adam to respond to Him? When Adam had fully considered God's words, he would have to decide to make what God had said a part of his life. If Adam simply heard God's words without attempting to apply them to his own life, he would not be relating to God as a person. If Adam failed at any point in that process, the relationship suffered. But if Adam carried the process through to the end, then his obedience formed a growing bond between himself and God.

QUESTION:
Why should I worship God?

PRINCIPLE 1:

A: God created me so that I could know Him and love Him. Worship flows from my love relationship with God.

We call this growing bond a relationship. No animal can truly relate the way humans can relate. This is part of what it means to be created in God's image.

The relational process is dangerous, however. The sender of communication cannot control what happens inside the receiver. In the Garden of Eden, God gave His will and allowed Adam to relate to it. In the end, Adam did not take into his heart what God had said, nor did he act on it. The relationship died. Adam disobeyed because he chose not to believe what God had said to him.

Faith Is the Foundation of a Relationship with God

No one who reads the Bible would doubt that faith is critically important to carrying on a relationship with God. Hebrews tells us that "without faith it is impossible to please God, because anyone who comes to him must believe that he exists and that he rewards those who earnestly seek him" (Hebrews 11:6). Why is this?

Building blocks of faith. If we can trust a person to be consistent, then we will likely carry on a healthy relationship. If we believe that this person will carry out whatever he promises, then we can have confidence in our relationship. Proven liars leave little room for genuine relationships.

Steps of faith in a relationship also are based upon what we have observed about ourselves, our world, our experiences and our understanding of those things. Once we act on our faith, we commit ourselves, making ourselves vulnerable. That commitment is the heart of every meaningful relationship.

Action and faith. Stepping out in faith is necessary to prove that our faith in any relationship is real. Yet it can be a frightening and dangerous act. If you were struggling with a secret sin, would you tell your best friend? If not, why not? Would you fear that you might not be able to trust your friend? By giving in to such fear, we are tacitly confessing that we cannot trust that person enough to take the risk. When we refuse to open up to others those secret parts of our lives, we are saying with our actions that we do not trust them.

What is true about our relationships with others is also true about our relationship with God. We need knowledge to strengthen faith—knowledge about what God is like, what He has promised, how He works and what He commands. We need two-way communication with Him: from Him to us through His Word, and from us to Him through prayer. In addition, we need the experience that comes from acting upon what we know and understand about Him. Without stepping out in action, our faith is dead (James 2:17).

This level of trust is necessary for any human relationship to flourish, and this level of faith is necessary for a genuine relationship with God. Therefore, this principle of faith is always necessary in worship as well, because worship begins with a relationship, and faith is the foundation of all relationships.

Faith is not simply the fact that we believe something to be so. Faith is believing something enough to step out in action because of it. Many Christians are convinced that their faith is mediocre because they do not have the level of passion that they see in other believers. They are looking at emotional faith, which may not have anything to do with true faith. The real question for all Christians is not how they feel about God, but how they live in their relationship with Him.

This is why the content of our worship—what we understand about God and His promises—is so important in worship. We need to know what God has said about Himself and His promises; otherwise, we will be unable to step out in faith. Without that faith, we will not be able to love God.

God created humankind to carry on a relationship with Him. The relationship always comes first. Jesus tells us that all of the Law, including the command to worship, depends on the commandment to love God with all our heart, soul and mind (Matthew 22:37-40). Until we love God, our worship is meaningless.

*   *   *

Pastor Jeff watched Troy leading the congregation in the opening hymn. He could feel the tension choking the singing, turning a beautiful hymn into a meaningless ritual. The three choruses they sang were no better. As the congregation sang the last words of the final chorus, Pastor Jeff thought to himself, *That was not worship.*

Jeff knew that before First Community Church could properly worship God, the church had to learn to love Him. The most difficult cure, loving God, was nevertheless the only remedy for the church's sickness.

As he closed the service in prayer, Jeff brought his own plea to God. "Lord, give us wisdom to learn to love You. Teach us how to love one another."

QUESTION:
Why should I worship God?

PRINCIPLE 1:

B: All relationships are based on trust. In my worship, I step out and trust what God has said about Himself and His ways.

Sin Destroys Love and Worship

Wednesday evening choir practice, February 7

Fred was already sitting in the choir room when Troy arrived for practice.

"Good evening, Troy. I thought I'd stop by early. I'd like to talk to you about something."

Troy shook Fred's hand and sat down in a chair across from him. He smiled. "Sure, Fred. What do you want to talk about?"

A troubled look clouded Fred's face. "I have a deep burden for this church. You know, we were a part of the original Bible study in Harold Miller's house thirty years ago. We didn't have a building, a pastor, or anything. And now . . ."

Fred stared at his hands. "I'm kinda worried about what's going to happen next. I'm afraid that we're going to lose our church. We . . ." He paused for a moment. His expression revealed his anxiety. Troy's stomach knotted. He had expected to face the conflict, but hardly so soon.

"What do you want to know?" Troy asked.

Fred nervously cleared his throat. "It's about all of this music stuff. Our church had been doing really well the past ten years or so. Then Rick came in, with his choruses and drums and raising hands." Fred looked up. "Troy, we just want to know where you are going to take us with this contemporary worship stuff."

Troy's stomach began churning. "We?"

Fred looked out the window. "You know, the people who feel like worship has been getting out of hand in this church. The people who really know what this church is all about."

And so it came out. Pastor Jeff had told Troy that Rick's style of worship had appalled many of the board members. They had run Pastor Rick from the church. A few even spoke against hiring another pastor of worship. Now Troy realized that Fred was a part of that group.

Troy looked at the window. A car had pulled in and he could see that Charles was getting out. He knew that Charles was Pastor Rick's biggest supporter. He had to finish this conversation before Charles walked in. He looked back at Fred.

"Fred, what do you mean that you're 'kinda worried'?"

Fred got up and walked slowly toward the conductor's podium. He picked up a pencil and began nonchalantly tapping the podium with it. "Troy, when the board tried to stop Pastor Rick from changing our worship, he fought them. Finally, they just had to get rid of him. I mean, they brought accusations to the congregation. They called for a vote. It was downright nasty."

Troy's mind raced through Pastor Jeff's stories about how nasty it actually was. Stories about late-night board meetings without the pastor and without certain "soft" board members. Stories about gossip, exaggerations, outright lies and threatening letters.

Troy looked Fred straight in the eyes. "I've heard that Rick's ministry was destroyed in this whole thing. I've heard that this church really hurt him and his family. They still haven't recovered."

Fred looked at the pencil, then slowly placed it back on the podium. After a long moment, he sighed. "Well, Troy . . . I guess that's all I needed to say." He moved toward the door and reached for the handle.

With a dejected smile, Fred spoke. "Thanks for listening." He pulled the door open and almost bumped into Charles.

Charles frowned. "Evening, Fred."

Fred said nothing and walked out.

* * *

When churches encounter worship wars, sin, not style, is the real problem. Rick brought a new worship style to the church. To "fix" what he perceived as the problem, Fred decided that he had to resort to desperate measures. Those measures were sometimes sinful. Once sin entered the process, it dominated everything else that happened.

Fred never admitted his sin, but continued to come to church every week. He apparently never questioned whether it was wrong for him to sing the hymns he had brought back into the worship service. He was ignoring the sins he had committed against the church.

Sin stops relationships. Fred needed to understand that sin makes worship impossible. First, it brings the relationship process to a halt. In Adam's case, he refused to hear God's words, treasure them and act on them. Once he refused to listen to God's command, Adam stopped relating to God.

Sin always leads to fear. The first human sin provides us with the best example of how sin also leads to unhealthy fear. After they sinned, Adam and Eve hid themselves. Why? They were afraid. "[Adam] answered, 'I heard you in the garden, and I was afraid because I was naked; so I hid' " (Genesis 3:10). Adam feared God, because he knew that God would punish his sin. John wrote that "fear has to do with punishment. The one who fears is not made perfect in love" (1 John 4:18). Sin transforms our longing for God into terror of His judgment. That kind of terror does not prepare us for authentic worship.

Those who sin hide from God. After he sinned, Adam hid from God in several ways. In addition to hiding physically, Adam hid his sin emotionally by transferring his fear. He should have been afraid that God would punish him because he had disobeyed Him. Instead, he feared that God would punish him for being naked. He transferred his guilt from the real issue—disobedience, lack of trust, turning from love and seeking his own will—to a very secondary (and incorrect) issue—nakedness. Worshipers around the world follow in Adam's footsteps.

They fear God for all of the wrong reasons, rather than facing the primary one: They have sinned against their Creator.

Relationally, Adam hid from God by blaming his sin on God and Eve. God asked Adam if he had disobeyed. He responded, "The woman you put here with me—she gave me some fruit from the tree, and I ate it" (Genesis 3:12). Adam may have convinced himself that Eve was the real culprit. Worse, Adam indirectly accused God of strapping him with this troublesome woman. He was sure that he himself was not to blame.

Sin drives people to lie about their sin, to blame others for their sin, to ignore their sin and to transfer their guilt to another unimportant problem. People with unconfessed sin in their lives still want to worship, but they do not want to face their sin. That creates an impossible dilemma. By denying their sin, they are building a wall against hearing what God might have to say about that one particular sinful attitude or action. They may want to know Him in the other "safe" areas, but they do not want Him to interfere with their sin. They approach God like a man approaches a prostitute, as someone to use and then discard. They hope to have the part of Him that does not demand their full love and full obedience.

That approach cannot work, because God is a whole person. We cannot use Him as if He were simply a means to an end. We must relate to Him as a person, considering what He says and applying it to our lives because we love Him. Without that response, what kind of relationship could we ever have? We cannot deny our sin and maintain a real relationship with God.

Satan works to destroy true worship. Satan also had a part to play in this drama. When he deceived Eve, she believed his lies. She even acted upon them, to her eternal regret. How ironic it is that Eve trusted Satan—someone she could not have a relationship with, because no relationship can be built on lies. Once she sinned, she could not have a relationship with God either, because her sin destroyed the process of growing in relationship. As Isaiah 59:2 says, "But your iniquities have separated you from your God; your sins have hidden his face from you, so that he will not hear." Worse yet, her fear drove her to hide from Him and to lie to herself and everyone else about her sin.

Satan, as the father of lies, works hard to make us his willing children. Jesus said,

> You belong to your father, the devil, and you want to carry out your father's desire. He was a murderer from the beginning, not holding to the truth, for there is no truth in him. When he lies, he speaks his native language, for he is a liar and the father of lies. (John 8:44)

*   *   *

Troy left the room and looked down the hallway. Fred was walking through the church exit. His heart sank. *What will I do, Lord?* he silently prayed. *This whole thing has nothing to do with music. It's all about sin.* Fred got what he wanted, Lord, but not really. Now he's doing it all over again, this time with me. Please give me wisdom.

Troy shook his head as he stood staring at the closed exit door. There were no winners in this struggle. Fred would keep on singing his traditional hymns without guilt because he refused to admit that he had sinned. He was hiding from

God. That made his worship meaningless. Worse yet, Troy
could not help him until Fred faced what he had done. The
entire church was going to suffer, and there was almost
nothing Troy could do about it.

QUESTION:
Why should I worship God?

PRINCIPLE 1:

C: When I sin, I am refusing to love God and
therefore cannot worship Him. My sin also drives
me to hide from Him.

T W O

Why Do I Bring
Offerings to God
in My Worship?

QUESTION:
Why do I bring offerings to God in my worship?

PRINCIPLE 2:

I bring God offerings as a way to present myself to
Him, asking Him to accept me as His servant.

QUESTION:
What makes my worship acceptable to God?

PRINCIPLE 3:

God accepts my worship only if my heart is genuine
before Him.

Continuation of Wednesday evening choir practice, February 7

All of the choir members sorted through their music while Troy made his way up to the front of the room.

"OK, everyone, let's get started."

Isabelle silently prayed for what was about to happen.

Troy calmed his heart and began to speak. "I've decided that we're going to spend some time every practice studying what the Bible teaches about worship."

Charles burst out passionately, "It's about time!"

Troy stole a quick glance at Fred's chair. It was still empty. He walked up to the white board and picked up a marker. "OK . . . let's have some ideas about what is the heart of worship."

Jerry raised his hand. "Singing songs that have meaning and depth to them."

Troy wrote it down on the board.

Bob added, "Prayer."

Joan called out, "Scripture reading."

Charles exclaimed, "I don't think any of that is the heart of worship! Worship is all about experiencing God's presence."

Penny quickly agreed. "Charles is right. Just because we sing a hymn or chorus, that doesn't mean that we are worshiping. We worship when we touch God. Worship is all about God."

Isabelle prayed fervently, *Lord, please help Troy to keep things under control.*

Troy stopped writing. He looked out over the twenty-five people sitting there and saw tension growing. It was now or never. He wrote the word *minhah* on the board. "Does anyone know what this word means?"

*   *   *

The Meaning of Bringing Offerings

Genesis tells us that long after God expelled Adam and Eve from Eden, their sons, Cain and Abel, brought offerings to God. Cain's offering came from his crops. The Hebrew language used in Genesis describes his gift as a *minhah*, and it was probably a grain offering. Later, the Law of Moses established the grain offering as an important part of Israel's worship. It was "a most holy part of the offerings made to the LORD by fire" (Leviticus 2:3). When Cain brought his grain, he was bringing an offering that normally would have pleased God.

Abel brought the firstlings of his flock and their fat portions. Genesis also describes Abel's offering as a *minhah*. "The LORD looked with favor on Abel and his offering (*minhah*)" (Genesis 4:4). Normally, writers of the Old Testament used different words to describe animal sacrifices from non-animal sacrifices. In portraying Abel's sacrifice, however, Moses deliberately chose the same word he used to describe Cain's offering. Moses wanted his readers to focus on the *minhah* as the key to the story.

Originally, *minhah* was used to describe gifts, but not just any gift. The *minhah* was a social ceremony. People presented a *minhah* when they were attempting to establish or enhance a relationship between the giver and the receiver. For example, Jacob used a *minhah* to attempt to restore his broken relationship with his angry brother, Esau. He selected many animals from his flock as an enormous *minhah* to send ahead to Esau. Jacob reasoned, "I will pacify him with these gifts (*minhah*) I am sending on ahead; later, when I see him, perhaps he will receive me" (Genesis 32:20).

There are two sides to this social ceremony. First, the giver announces his inferior status and the receiver's superior status. Along with the gifts, he is presenting himself to the receiver as a subordinate. Second, the receiver chooses either to accept the gift or reject it. If the receiver rejects it, then he is rejecting the giver. In many cultures, such a response can lead to broken relationships or even war.

The only gift we have in America that comes close to a *minhah* is the engagement ring. Think of how profound a statement a man makes when he gives his girlfriend an engagement ring. Likewise, think of how profound a statement the woman makes when she accepts it. If she refuses the ring, she is refusing the proposal to bring their relationship to a new level. The ritual of presenting and accepting (or rejecting) the ring stands as the crossroads in courtship. The *minhah* serves the same kind of purpose, working as a tool to usher relationships into a new stage.

Now we understand why Cain and Abel brought *minhah* offerings to God that day. This was no simple ritual they were performing. Like a suitor offering a ring to his beloved, so Cain and Abel offered a *minhah* to God. They were presenting *themselves* to God and making a statement: "You are much greater than I, Lord. I formally request that You make me Your humble servant. Accept this offer of myself to You in this gift I am presenting."

In our story, the choir members did not understand the real meaning of worship. Troy knew that worship was not about singing, praying or even experiencing God's presence. We worship to remind ourselves and show God what we really want in our relationship with Him. We present ourselves along with our worship, telling God, "You are much greater than I, Lord. I ask

that You make me Your humble servant. Accept this offer of myself to You in this gift I am presenting."

*   *   *

Troy's lecture was obviously not working. The choir
looked at him with quizzical stares.

He asked, "Think about the *minhah* offering. What was
the most important part of it?"

Most choir members still looked puzzled. A couple members on both sides were scowling. Troy worried that the
whole experiment was going to die.

Quietly Marcia raised her hand. She was afraid to answer
Troy because of all the controversy that had been choking
their church. Marcia felt that she had been trapped between two warring armies. She hadn't been thrilled with everything Pastor Rick had changed, but she also was sure that
the board had sinned in the way the members treated him.
Yet Marcia wanted to help Troy out, at least to give him a
fighting chance to help the church survive the conflict they
were experiencing.

Troy called on Marcia.

She paused, then cautiously answered, "The *minhah* was
like a relationship, wasn't it? The worshiper was asking God
to accept him." Marcia paused for a moment and then
added, "It was almost like a proposal."

Silently, Troy thanked God for enabling Marcia to give
the right answer.

He prodded her further. "Marcia, what do you think was
the most important part of the *minhah*?"

The room became very quiet as Marcia struggled to put it
into words. Suddenly, her face lit up. "Whether or not he
really meant it."

"Meant what?"

She smiled. "Whether or not the worshiper really wanted to be God's servant."

Q U E S T I O N :
Why do I bring offerings to God in my worship?

P R I N C I P L E   2 :

I bring God offerings as a way to present myself to Him, asking Him to accept me as His servant.

The First Worship Accepted . . . and Rejected

Continuation of Wednesday evening choir practice, February 7

Troy looked around the room to see how people were responding to Marcia's answer.

Charles looked puzzled. "Troy, I guess I don't understand what this *minhah* offering has to do with worship. Worship is more than that, isn't it?"

Troy stopped and thought. In one sense, Charles was right. Yet the deeper one went into worship, the more one realized that worship is far more than what Charles conveyed.

Troy smiled. "Charles, let me give you an example." He turned to Isabelle. "Sweetheart, what was the most romantic thing we ever did together?"

Isabelle didn't hesitate. "That's easy. Those two weeks we spent trail riding in Banff National Park."

Troy nodded. "OK. What is the most important thing we ever did for our romantic relationship?"

The question baffled Isabelle. She had no idea what he wanted her to say. She paused for a long moment and decided to say what really mattered to her. "I don't know. I guess our decision to spend at least one evening every week just talking together about anything we wanted to bring up."

Troy laughed. "There's nothing romantic about most of those evenings, I can tell you. We talk about the kids, about repairing our car and our broken-down lawnmower. Sometimes we deal with some pretty tense topics. But I agree with Isabelle. We build our relationship on Tuesday evenings during our talk time. That's more important for our romance than the romance itself. I'm sure you women understand what I mean."

Janice immediately agreed. "Men are always trying to create a special mood for romance. It's hard for wives to get into a romantic mood when their husbands have been ignoring them all week."

Christine jumped in. "That's for sure. Romance is fun, but for me, the relationship is by far more important."

Troy looked at Charles. "Charles, do you see what I mean? God really doesn't care that much about our worship. He cares about our relationship with Him."

Charles frowned. He looked as if he was trying to figure out what Troy was really saying, but also as if he was threatened by it. Although Charles did not respond, others seemed to understand what Troy was saying. In fact, the tension in the room seemed to ease. Isabelle breathed a prayer of thanks. They had just taken a first step toward healing the church.

*　*　*

Why did God reject Cain's minhah? We can imagine that the first recorded offering happened something like this. Cain approached and laid his *minhah* on the altar. He bowed, backed off and waited. Then Abel brought his *minhah*, laid it on the altar, bowed and backed off.

Then God spoke. "Abel, I am pleased with your *minhah*. I accept you and your gift." Abel smiled.

God continued. "Cain, your *minhah* displeases Me. I do not accept either you or your gift." Cain grimaced in anger. "Then the LORD said to Cain, 'Why are you angry? Why is your face downcast? If you do what is right, will you not be accepted? But if you do not do what is right, sin is crouching at your door; it desires to have you, but you must master it' " (Genesis 4:6-7). God rejected Cain's appeal for His approval by rejecting Cain's *minhah*.

Thousands of times a day around the world people go through a social gift ritual similar to the *minhah* offering. In each instance, the receiver decides whether to accept the gift and the giver, or to reject the offer. In this story, God had no favor for Cain and therefore rejected his gift.

Why did God reject Cain and his offering? The biblical account shows us that an evil heart had led Cain to present the *minhah*. His entire relationship with God was at stake. Remember the image of the suitor proposing marriage? He asks her to marry him by giving his beloved an engagement ring. The *minhah* had that kind of investment in it. Yet when God rejected the *minhah*, Cain did not attempt to repair the relationship. Instead, he lashed out in a murderous rage. His heart was obviously corrupted.

What drove Cain to strike out in anger? First John 3:12 tells us that Cain was already deeply entrenched in sin. "Do not be like Cain, who belonged to the evil one and murdered his brother. And why did he murder him? Because his own actions were evil and his brother's were righteous." The original language of this passage indicates that Cain's deeds were *habitually* evil. He murdered his brother because of a *lifestyle* of sinning. Probably all along Abel's righteous attitudes and behavior had been making Cain feel guilty about his own sinful behavior. Cain knew that he was wrong, but he did not repent. Long before God rejected his *minhah* that day, Cain had been hardening his heart to what he knew was right. He wanted to keep on sinning. He murdered his brother to hide from his own sin. Abel's righteous deeds condemned him, and the only way to stop the condemnation was to kill Abel.

What did John mean when he said that Cain "belonged to the evil one"? To answer that, let's review what Eve did. Rather than hearing God's word, considering it, making it her own and acting on it, she embraced Satan's words. Satan was a liar. No one can build a real relationship upon lies. Eve embraced Satan and became his pawn. Cain did the same.

We know that Cain wanted God's favor. Otherwise, he would not have wasted his offering. He presented his *minhah* in hopes that God would accept him. For Cain, however, the *minhah* was simply a way of hiding from God. He used the *minhah* as a smoke screen to cover his evil deeds. Cain had no more intention of growing in a love relationship with God than did Satan.

The story of Cain illustrates one of worship's foundational principles. God does not look at the outward gift, but instead looks at the heart of the giver. We cannot live Cain's lifestyle Monday through Saturday and then expect somehow to present Abel's offering on Sunday. When someone brings God an offering of worship, he is saying that he intends to grow in his relationship with God. Without the relationship, the worship is simply a ritual.

*   *   *

Charles and Sharlene pulled out of the church parking lot. Sharlene looked very carefully at her silent husband. She could sense a battle raging within him.

"What's bothering you, Charles? Is it Troy's devotional?"

He wearily shook his head. "What did Troy mean about that *minhah* lesson? Did you hear what he said? He said that God doesn't care about worship! What is he trying to do? I don't know what's going on, Sharlene. When I got to choir practice, Troy was there buddying up with Fred. I've got a very bad feeling that this thing is going to get worse."

Sharlene looked at her husband with a curious expression. "Charles, you need to give Troy a chance. He just arrived here. He's probably just trying to feel out the choir and figure out where everyone is."

Charles frowned. "Did you see the way Troy went after me in our discussion time? He's doing more than feeling the choir out. He's made a decision. Troy is giving in to the board."

Sharlene paused. Troy seemed nice enough, but the last four months had shown them how even close friends can turn to enemies over an issue as charged as music. She couldn't be sure of anything at this point. Maybe Charles was right.

Charles turned the corner onto their street. Worry gnawed within his heart. What else could he do? He had done everything he could to support Rick, and that was a disaster. He didn't want another war and he didn't trust Troy.

QUESTION:
What makes my worship acceptable to God?

PRINCIPLE 3:

God accepts my worship only if my heart is genuine before Him.

THREE

Why Did the Old Testament Require Animal Sacrifices in Worship?

QUESTION:
Why did the Old Testament
require animal sacrifices in worship?

PRINCIPLE 4:

Worshipers brought animal sacrifices so that God's
wrath might fall on the sacrifice rather than on the
sinner. The sacrifice was a picture of what God
would later do to Jesus Christ, the true Lamb of God.

Why Did the Old Testament Require Animal Sacrifices in Worship?

Pastor's office, Thursday morning, February 8

Troy dropped into the seat across from Pastor Jeff and sighed.

Jeff looked up. "How did choir practice go last night?"

Troy ran his fingers through his hair. "I just don't know. It was really tense. Fred walked out before practice started. Charles acted as if I were his enemy." He looked down at the desk in discouragement. "Maybe I made a mistake in coming here."

Troy's look told it all. Jeff had warned him about the battles. He himself was already discouraged. He could imagine how difficult it would be for a new worship director to come into First Community Church's worship war. His mind raced through a dozen answers, but none were appropriate. He carefully watched Troy's expression and slowly came to realize that Troy had more to say, but was holding back.

"Troy, there's something else, isn't there?"

Troy began slowly. "Well . . . this whole worship war stinks. A lot of these people have sinned. The whole church is a mess. We need to start over again, from the beginning."

Jeff looked surprised. "What do you mean, 'start over'?"

Troy nervously cleared his throat and began what seemed to be a prepared speech. "The songs we sing on Sunday mornings are meaningless because we are not loving each other. That makes our worship an insult to God. It doesn't matter if we sing hymns or choruses or Handel's *Messiah*." He leaned forward, looking the senior pastor in the eye. "Until this congregation repents of sin, we might as well not even sing."

Jeff looked away. He knew how important repentance was for turning the church around. But nobody could force this congregation to face its sin and turn away from it. Only God could change their hearts. Troy was expecting a miracle.

Jeff shook his head. "Troy, what do you think we should do?"

The worship leader had an answer ready. "This Sunday is communion Sunday. Let's focus the entire service on communion. Let's drop the singing. No hymns. No choruses. No special music." He picked up Jeff's Bible and flipped through the pages to First Corinthians 11. "Listen to this:

> For whenever you eat this bread and drink this cup, you proclaim the Lord's death until he comes.
>
> Therefore, whoever eats the bread or drinks the cup of the Lord in an unworthy manner will be guilty of sinning against the body and blood of the Lord. A man ought to examine himself before he eats of the bread and drinks of the cup. For anyone who eats and drinks without recognizing the body of the Lord eats and drinks judgment on himself. That is why many among you are weak and sick, and a number of you have fallen asleep. But if we judged ourselves, we would not come under judgment. When we are judged by the Lord, we are being disciplined so that we will not be condemned with the world.
>
> So then, my brothers, when you come together to eat, wait for each other. (11:26-33)

"Jeff, that's what this congregation needs to hear. We need to hear that God does not want our music as long as we keep on sinning against each other. You've got to bring this whole congregation back to basics so that later on we can try to fix our worship problems. First things first. It's time to deal with our sin."

Jeff nodded. He knew Troy was right, but that did not make him feel any better. Nobody wanted to hear what Troy was saying. He was not looking forward to preaching a message on repentance when the church was about to go up in flames.

*   *   *

Substitution

How Can Sinners Approach a Holy God?

Troy realized that sin stands as an impenetrable barrier between God and those who attempt to bring Him worship. No one can approach the Holy God with even a taint of sin. Sin blocks the way to God because sin at its heart rejects God. Sinners do not wish to know God; they wish to sin. They do not want to love God; they want to love themselves. Therefore, sin makes a real relationship with God impossible.

How sinful Noah could worship the Holy God. The story of Noah proves that God does not take sin lightly. God responded to humanity's sin by wiping out the human race.

> The LORD saw how great man's wickedness on the earth had become, and that every inclination of the thoughts of his heart was only evil all the time. The LORD was grieved that he had made man on the earth, and his heart was filled with pain. So the LORD said, "I will wipe mankind, whom I have created, from the face of the earth—men and animals, and creatures that move along the ground, and birds

of the air—for I am grieved that I have made them."
(Genesis 6:5-7)

Sin brings death and ultimately eternal punishment.
Sin also bars the way to God, and no good deeds, including sincere worship, can overcome it. Yet we have
already seen that God accepted the worship offered by
sinners. God received Abel's worship, even though Abel
surely sinned. God also received Noah's worship in
Genesis 8:20-21, even though we know from Noah's
life that he was less than perfect (9:21). How could a
holy God accept offerings when sinful men presented
them?
   The answer lies in the kind of sacrifice Noah brought.

> Then Noah built an altar to the LORD and, taking
> some of all the clean animals and clean birds, he sac-
> rificed burnt offerings on it. The LORD smelled the
> pleasing aroma and said in his heart: "Never again
> will I curse the ground because of man, even though
> every inclination of his heart is evil from childhood.
> And never again will I destroy all living creatures, as I
> have done." (8:20-21)

There was something about Noah's sacrifice that
changed God's mind. Without its soothing aroma, God
would not have received Noah's gift. Without that sacrifice, He would have flooded the earth again.
   Noah's sacrifice was an 'ola, a whole burnt sacrifice.
The 'ola was a very special sacrifice. Leviticus carefully describes God's requirements for the 'ola offering. The worshiper would bring an animal without defect (Leviticus
1:3) and "lay his hand on the head of the burnt offering,
and it [would] be accepted on his behalf to make atone-

ment for him" (1:4). By laying his hand on the animal, the worshiper was saying that he was a sinner and ought to die, but the animal was dying in his place. The worshiper would then put the animal to death. "He is to slaughter the young bull before the LORD" (1:5). The worshiper did all of the gruesome work. He skinned it: "He is to skin the burnt offering and cut it into pieces" (1:6). He gutted it and washed the legs and entrails: "He is to wash the inner parts and the legs with water" (1:9). After the worshiper finished the dirty work, the priest would completely burn the animal, so that nothing of it would be left.

The 'ola was anything but an inspiring experience for the worshiper. Every part of it was distasteful. God designed the 'ola to be offensive because sin itself is detestable. Finding relief from sin through the 'ola was bloody work. The entire act became a visceral experience of death. Noah's offering of worship was a very gruesome event, a bitter taste of death. In our story, Troy had begun to realize that his new congregation had lost that bitter taste in worshiping God, the taste that comes when we face our sin and its awful consequences, the taste of death that was a vital part of Hebrew worship.

The story of Noah does not explain how that 'ola could cleanse a human from sin. After all, we sin against our relationship with God. We reject Him when we sin. How could killing a dumb animal bring life to our broken relationship? Yet Noah's 'ola sacrifice actually turned away God's wrath for sin.

We could ask the same question about worship at First Community Church. How could any songs of worship break through the wall that their sins against God had built? The congregation was entrapped in hatred and mistrust. The people were battling over, of all things, what was the right way to worship God. How could they feel good about bringing offerings of praise when their sins were blocking the way to the throne? They somehow assumed that singing joyful songs would erase the stench of their sin, but it could not. A deeper answer must explain how a sinner such as Noah or any one of those at First Community Church could come before the living God.

Why Abraham's son needed an 'ola. Like Noah, the story of Abraham centers on the 'ola sacrifice. God called Abraham to offer his son Isaac as an 'ola.

> Some time later God tested Abraham. He said to him, "Abraham!"
>
> "Here I am," he replied.
>
> Then God said, "Take your son, your only son, Isaac, whom you love, and go to the region of Moriah. Sacrifice him there as a burnt offering on one of the mountains I will tell you about." (Genesis 22:1-2)

God commanded Abraham to slay his son and then completely consume him in flames so that only Isaac's ashes would remain.

Abraham was to present the 'ola as an offering of worship. The word _worship_ appears for the first time in the Bible in this passage. "[Abraham] said to his servants, 'Stay here with the donkey while I and the boy go over there. We will worship and then we will come back to you'" (22:5).

Isaac understood what Abraham meant when he said that they were going to worship. "As the two of them went on together, Isaac spoke up and said to his father Abraham, 'Father?' 'Yes, my son?' . . . 'The fire and the wood are here,' Isaac said, 'but where is the lamb for the burnt offering?' " (22:6-7). The son understood that real worship required a distasteful and blood-filled sacrifice.

They arrived on Mount Moriah and Abraham prepared his son for death. But the moment before Abraham would have killed his beloved son, God intervened. He sent a ram to take Isaac's place.

> But the angel of the LORD called out to him from heaven, "Abraham, Abraham!"
>
> "Here I am," he replied.
>
> "Do not lay a hand on the boy," he said. "Do not do anything to him. Now I know that you fear God, because you have not withheld from me your son, your only son."
>
> Abraham looked up and there in a thicket he saw a ram caught by its horns. He went over and took the ram and sacrificed it as a burnt offering instead of his son. So Abraham called that place The LORD Will Provide. And to this day it is said, "On the mountain of the LORD it will be provided." (22:11-14)

Isaac should have died. God, however, provided an innocent victim to take Isaac's place. That was the point of the 'ola sacrifice. The sinner placed his hands upon the victim to symbolically transfer his sins from himself to the animal. He was then to slay the animal as a substitute for himself.

How could the death of a ram undo the penalty of Abraham's many sins against God? Abraham gave us a key when he named that place, "The LORD Will Provide." That mountain was the place where God provided deliverance for Isaac. "On the mountain of the LORD it will be provided." Redemption from sin came to Isaac on the mount of the Lord, Mount Moriah.

Moriah, the place where Solomon built his temple (2 Chronicles 3:1). Moriah, the home of Herod's temple, a glorious remodeling of Zerubbabel's temple (built during Ezra's day). Moriah, the mount where Jesus taught as a young child and as a young man, and later chased out moneychangers, healed the blind, revealed His glory and unveiled His goodness.

And outside the walls of the city, on Mount Moriah, Jesus of Nazareth stumbled toward the place of His death. They had beaten His face until it was battered and bloody. They had shredded His back with a scourge. They had gashed His head with their crown of thorns. And there, on Mount Moriah, they crucified Him as a bloody sacrifice, a detestable offering. That day Mount Moriah saw only death. Sinners laid their hands on their innocent Victim. Sinners sacrificed Him in a gruesome act of hatred.

There was nothing lovely about Mount Moriah that day. Nothing sweet, nothing stirring. It was a bitter mountain, a mountain of death.

Yet Moriah is the mountain of our worship. It was always so. Moriah was the mountain of Abraham's worship. There he brought Isaac as his *'ola* offering. Moriah was the mountain of Jesus' worship. There He presented Himself as a bloody and bitter *'ola* sacrifice. There on that mountain He took the sinner's place. Moriah is the mountain of all true worship, for on Moriah God provided His only beloved Son, Jesus, as the final *'ola*, the final sacrifice.

Noah's bloody *'ola* was a picture of Jesus. Abraham's bloody *'ola* was a picture of Jesus. The hundreds of thousands of bloody *'ola* offerings presented in the temple were all pictures of Jesus. They were gruesome rituals, because Jesus' death was an appalling spectacle. We come to bring God worship through that gruesome death. We do not reach God through our praises. We do not meet Him through our prayers. We do not touch Him through our songs. We come to Him at the cross, on Mount Moriah. "On the mountain of the LORD it will be provided" (Genesis 22:14). Moriah, the Mount of Crucifixion, is the mountain of our worship.

In our story, Troy began to realize that his new congregation had lost that bitter taste in worshiping God, the taste that comes when we face our sin and its awful consequences, a taste of death that was so much a part of Hebrew worship. Troy's congregation had forgotten that they must come to God in the shadow of the cross. They must meet God on Mount Moriah.

* * *

Sunday morning service, February 11

Pastor Jeff sat after preaching the most important message of his ministry. His text had been First Corinthians 11:17-34, on the Lord's Supper. The heart of the message was, "Don't take communion until you have dealt with your sin."

Now the elders were serving communion and the pastor looked out over the congregation. So far, everyone had taken the bread from the plate. It was almost as if nobody had even heard the sermon. He bent his head in sorrow and began to pray.

Jeff heard someone stirring in the pews. When he looked up, he expected to see Charles or Fred, but neither had moved. It was Hazel, an eighty-seven-year-old saint of God, who was slowly and painfully making her way down the aisle toward the altar. Hazel, the godliest, kindest saint Jeff had ever known, was coming forward.

He sat in profound disappointment. Hazel was the last person who needed to repent. After a few moments, however, he quietly walked over to the front pew where Hazel was sitting. She looked up, tears filling her eyes.

"Pastor," she said in a quiet voice, "I have sinned against the Lord." Hazel paused, the tears now flowing freely. "I was so glad when the board removed Pastor Rick. I was so glad because I didn't want things to change from the way they had always been. The whole time I knew deep down that I was sinning against Rick in my heart. I just didn't want to think about it, until you preached this morning. I held this bread and thought about Jesus' sufferings. I thought about how He forgave the Pharisees and the soldiers. How He was willing to suffer because He loved them. And then I realized that I couldn't eat communion . . . not until I got my heart right with the Lord."

Hazel's words pierced Jeff's heart. He suddenly faced the deep scars of bitterness he had been harboring against those who fired Rick. He suddenly saw the horror of his own sins and knew why nobody had responded to his message. Jeff himself had to respond. Only then could his congregation follow. Slowly, Jeff found himself kneeling beside Hazel, tears now running down his own face.

And there they stayed. Both of them silently praying for God to work in their lives. Both of them asking God to soften their hard hearts. Both of them looking to the cross for healing,

QUESTION:
Why did the Old Testament
require animal sacrifices in worship?

PRINCIPLE 4:

> Worshipers brought animal sacrifices so that
> God's wrath might fall on the sacrifice rather than
> on the sinner. The sacrifice was a picture of what
> God would later do to Jesus Christ, the true Lamb
> of God.

cleansing and restoration. Both of them looking to Jesus'
blood to wash them and renew them. Both of them realizing,
at last, that only Jesus' blood can cleanse such sin.

FOUR

According to Moses, What Does God Require of Me for Worship?

QUESTION:
According to Moses, what does God
require of me for worship?

PRINCIPLE 5:

A: According to Moses, God requires me to put myself in my proper relationship with Him.

QUESTION:
According to Moses, what did God
require of Israel for worship?

B: According to Moses, God required Israel to serve
Him with all of their hearts through offerings and
sacrifice.

QUESTION:
According to Moses, how did
music relate to Israel's worship?

C: God did not reveal to Moses what part music was
to play in Israel's worship.

QUESTION:
According to Moses, what else did God
require of Israel for worship?

D: According to Moses, God required Israel to worship Him by remembering His mighty saving acts.

Staff meeting, Tuesday morning, February 13

"Nobody moved." Jeff sat at his office desk, a dejected look on his face.

Troy sat across from him, but said nothing.

"Nobody moved. Except for Hazel, nobody even heard what I said, Troy."

It was a time for listening. Troy simply nodded.

Jeff stared at his hands and muttered. "Why did they even come to worship?"

Silence lingered for what seemed to be an eternity. Troy was conflicted. He wanted to listen patiently to his friend, yet also wanted so much to answer Jeff's questions. Finally his impatience won. "Jeff, they weren't coming to worship. They were just plain coming to church."

Jeff looked up in surprise. He thought for a moment before speaking. "What do you mean by that?"

Troy replied carefully. "I just don't think our congregation understands what worship is all about."

Jeff shook his head. "I disagree, Troy. We went through a two-month Sunday evening series on worship last year."

Troy frowned. He could keep silent and avoid causing Pastor Jeff more pain, or he could tell him what was really on his heart. *Oh, well,* he thought, *better cause the pain now than later.* He said a quick prayer and began to speak. "You know, Jeff, people think that they're worshiping God when they sing 'Holy, Holy, Holy' or 'It's All about You, Lord.' Worship is a lot different from that. The whole idea of worship deals with straightening out our relationship with God."

Jeff immediately disagreed. "Troy, the word *worship* means to ascribe worth to God. It's about giving God His due."

Troy shook his head. "No, that's what it means in Middle English. In Hebrew it means to bow at the waist before someone. In Greek it means to prostrate yourself before someone."

Jeff could not understand what Troy was driving at. "So? What does that have to do with worship? Bowing is just a ritual."

Troy stopped for a moment. This was turning into an argument—and that was the last thing First Community Church needed. He decided to take a different approach. "Jeff, why were you weeping during the communion service?"

Jeff could see the earnestness on his friend's face and knew that Troy was not trying to pick a fight. He thought for a moment and then spoke. "I knew I was being a hypocrite. I couldn't talk to them about taking communion the right way if I had unconfessed sin in my life."

Troy let that thought sink in for a moment and then said, "So, was that worship?"

Troy's question stopped Jeff cold. He thought very carefully, then said, "Yes, it was worship, I think."

Troy continued. "Was it the tears or the kneeling or the prayers you said?"

"None of those." Jeff thought about what had happened Sunday. "It was what was going on in my heart. I was getting things right with God."

Troy probed even deeper. "Did you worship God because of the communion service?"

Jeff considered for a long moment before he answered. "In a sense I did. I mean, I did not want to take communion until I had made things right. I wanted communion to be real."

Troy leaned back in his chair and asked his final question. He knew this would get to the heart of the matter. "Jeff, you've led communion a number of times since this wor-

ship war began. What made this communion service different from the others?"

Jeff thought long and hard. "This time I wasn't looking for
blessing. I was looking for cleansing. Once I talked to Hazel I
realized how wrong I was. I knew I had to make things
right."

Troy smiled. "That's what worship is, Jeff—getting your
walk with God where it's supposed to be."

* * *

Worship: A Balanced Relationship

When Jeff faced his own sin, he was ready to worship. The communion service, his prayers, his tears,
even his emotions were not worship. Jeff was worshiping God in the process of restoring his relationship with
the Lord. Worship in the Old and New Testaments
centers on our relationship with God.

What is worship in the Bible? The word often translated as "worship" in Hebrew (*shahah*) means to bow
down at the waist before someone. In Greek, the word
translated "worship" (*proskuneo*) means to lie on one's
face before someone. In both cases, those who worship
are making a relational statement about the person they
are worshiping.

If you were living in ancient Middle Eastern culture,
you would express your social standing by bowing or
prostrating yourself before other people. Bowing meant
placing yourself on a rank lower than the person before
you. It was a social statement. It also was a symbolic offering of your services, as a servant might offer them to
his master. Ancient Middle Eastern culture put great em-

phasis on maintaining the proper balance within the strata of society.

Americans have almost no ceremonies left (such as bowing) that define social relationships. In fact, theoretically in America we are not supposed to have any social classes at all. If we were in another culture, however, knowing our social relationships would tell us how we should act with another person. If, for example, an older person spoke, we who are younger would obey whatever he suggested, even if he were wrong. It would be a much greater cultural sin to disregard our elders than to obey his incorrect request. If our obedience to an older person resulted in a bad situation, our peers would respect us for our piety.

In the same way, if we were part of the lower castes of India, we would treat the higher castes with the highest of respect. No one in society would see this as a matter of custom. We would do this because proper behavior within classes and social ranks keeps society in what Hindus see as a spiritual balance. In Hindu society, the caste system is not just a social system but a spiritual reality. One rebellious act unbalances the caste system and subjects the whole community to spiritual suffering and bad karma.

The Hebrews bowed to those who possessed a higher rank. Joseph outraged his father and brothers because in his dream they bowed to him. Culturally, since he was the next-to-youngest son, they expected him to bow before them. "When he told his father as well as his brothers, his father rebuked him and said, 'What is this dream you had? Will your mother and I and your brothers actually come and bow down to the ground before you?'" (Genesis 37:10). When higher-ranking family members bowed before the next-to-youngest son, the family order went out of balance. This could be a grave cultural sin.

The Hebrews had all of this cultural background profoundly ingrained into their hearts. Thus, when in both the Old and New Testaments people worshiped the Lord by bowing, they were making a deep statement to God. "Then the man bowed down and worshiped the LORD" (Genesis 24:26). "[The people] believed. And when they heard that the LORD was concerned about them and had seen their misery, they bowed down and worshiped" (Exodus 4:31; see also Genesis 24:48; 47:31; Exodus 12:27; 34:8; 2 Chronicles 7:3; 20:18; 29:28-30; Nehemiah 8:6; Psalm 22:29 and 95:6). Within their cultural setting, they were saying to themselves and to God, "I myself know and I want You to know that I am in proper relationship with You." They were maintaining the correct balance with God.

Jeff had always thought that worship meant glorifying God or ascribing Him His worth. This is an American approach to worship. Worship becomes something we do *to* God. We magnify Him. We lift Him up. We glorify Him.

The social ritual of bowing, *shahah*, has a much different idea behind it. The Hebrew who bowed was realigning his relationship with One who is far greater. God's greatness was not the issue in *shahah*. The relationship was all-important. To glorify God or to ascribe Him worth simply tells how we *feel* about Him. To worship Him in a biblical way, we make sure that our lives are under His care and His lordship.

Shahah meant that worshipers knew how they should act toward their Lord. It was neither a mystical experience nor an emotional encounter. *Shahah* was an attempt to bring relational harmony between the King of the universe and those whom He had created in His image.

Christians in America assume that worship relates to singing and "experiencing God." Often Americans raise their hands to worship God, almost as if they are reaching out to Him and touching Him. For some, worship becomes an attempt to experience God, to know His presence. But in the historical books of the Old Testament (for example, Joshua 22:27; Judges 6:10; 1 Samuel 1:3; 1 Kings 1:47; 2 Kings 10:28; 2 Chronicles 29:28; and Ezra 7:19), the word *shahah* always indicates one of three things: (1) warnings against worshiping false gods; (2) presenting sacrifices and offerings to God in the tabernacle or temple; (3) bowing low before God, which usually happened at the temple.

Much of the warfare going on at First Community Church came from a false understanding of worship. Pastor Jeff began to understand this only when he thought about his own experience during the communion service.

*   *   *

Continuation of staff meeting, Tuesday morning, February 13

Jeff listened as Troy explained the Hebrew idea of bowing in worship. Step-by-step, Jeff began to see a way out of the bitter battle they were undergoing at First Community Church.

When Troy finished, he wondered whether he had convinced Jeff or lost him. After a few moments, Jeff smiled. "Troy, if we teach our congregation to worship God properly, this whole war will end. We've been fighting about the wrong things!"

Troy felt relieved. "There is hope, but it's going to be an uphill climb."

With a nod, Jeff agreed. "The climb is very steep, but at least we'll be going to higher ground. That's where we belong."

QUESTION:
According to Moses, what does God
require of me for worship?

PRINCIPLE 5:

A: According to Moses, God requires me to put myself in my proper relationship with Him.

Worship: Serving God Through Offerings and Sacrifices

Jeff and Troy talked through lunch. They traded Scripture passage after Scripture passage. The more Jeff thought about what Troy was saying, the more he began to find hope for First Community Church. The question was, how could they teach this to the congregation? They soon concluded that the choir was the key to bringing healing to the whole church. Some choir members had been committed to Pastor Rick, while others had actively worked to remove him. If God could bring healing to the choir, then the rest of the congregation would follow. They kept talking and thinking, thinking and talking.

Jeff came up with the idea first. Why not simply drop all music, including the choir? For three months, they would sing no hymns, no choruses and no special music. They would try to learn together what it meant to worship God.

Troy was glad that Jeff understood the problem, but he wondered if the senior pastor might have gone a little overboard. Who would go to a church with no singing? Besides, singing was not the problem—not understanding the true meaning of worship was.

That's when Jeff asked Troy for the passage on worship that had most spoken to his heart. Troy went over to Jeff's bookcase and pulled out an old, weathered Bible. He turned to Amos 5:21 and began to read. Halfway through, he stopped and handed the Bible to Jeff to finish.

> I hate, I despise your religious feasts;
>   I cannot stand your assemblies.
> Even though you bring me burnt offerings
>   and grain offerings,
>   I will not accept them.
> Though you bring choice fellowship offerings,
>   I will have no regard for them.
> Away with the noise of your songs!
>   I will not listen to the music of your harps.
> But let justice roll on like a river,
>   righteousness like a never-failing stream! (5:21-24)

Jeff closed the book. Tears filled his eyes. Troy bowed his head and both began to pray aloud, confessing, regretting, mourning their own sins and the sins of their church. After a long while of prayer, the two sat in prayerful silence, waiting on God.

*   *   *

Although the word *shahah* ("worship") did not speak to what the Hebrews were to *do* in worship, God did require them to *do* certain things. In our story, First Community Church had to do certain things in worship. They were to bring God offerings (2 Corinthians 8-9). They were to present themselves as living sacrifices (Romans 12:1-2). They were to "speak to one another with psalms, hymns and spiritual songs" and "sing and make music in [their] heart[s] to the Lord" (Ephesians 5:19). The Old Testament writers would not have described these activities with the word *shahah*. They would have used another word, *abad*, to describe the things God requires us to *do* unto Him. Next to *shahah*, this is perhaps the most important word to know in order to understand biblical worship.

The New American Standard Bible translates *abad* with the English word "worship" seven times. One instance is in Exodus 3:12: "And He said, 'Certainly I will be with you, and this shall be the sign to you that it is I who have sent you: when you have brought the people out of Egypt, you shall worship [*abad*] God at this mountain'" (NASB). The idea communicated through this word, however, is dramatically different from *shahah*.

Originally, the word *abad* described what a servant did for his master. But as time went on, the word also began to describe the *actions* of worship to any god, including the only true God, the Lord. True worshipers of God *served* [*abad*] Him, just as sinful idolaters *served* [*abad*] their idols. "You shall not worship their gods, nor serve [*abad*] them, nor do according to their deeds; but you shall utterly overthrow them and break their sacred pillars in pieces" (Exodus 23:24, NASB).

The word *shahah* meant bowing before God to show Him that the worshiper's relationship with God was in balance. The word *abad*, on the other hand, usually described the things worshipers did *unto* God (or idols). For example, the priests *served* (*abad*) the Lord by bringing Him sacrifices, incense and offerings. "It shall be a

witness between us and you and between our generations after us, that we are to perform the service of the
LORD before Him with our burnt offerings, and with
our sacrifices and with our peace offerings" (Joshua
22:27, NASB). Serving God had a religious sense to it,
because it did often describe the offerings and sacrifices
that God required Israel to present to Him.

The battle at First Community Church centered on
abad. Fred wanted to *do* certain kinds of things in worshiping God. Pastor Rick wanted to *do* other kinds of
things in worshiping God. The *doing* of worship was the
real controversy. Whether or not they raised their hands
was a question of what they were *doing*. The kind of music
they sang was a question of *doing*. Even the feelings they
created within themselves were a result of what they were
doing. Yet what they *did* in worship was not as important
as what they *were* when they did it. God's approach to
serving (*abad*) Him centered on the heart.

Worship: Serving God with All of Our Hearts

God did not want Israel's *abad*, their service, unless it
came from their *hearts*. Moses commanded the people to
serve God with all of their hearts. "And now, O Israel,
what does the LORD your God ask of you but to fear the
LORD your God, to walk in all his ways, to love him, to
serve the LORD your God with all your heart and with all
your soul" (Deuteronomy 10:12). God required that the
Israelites serve Him with all of their hearts and with all of
their souls.

The best way to understand this command is to examine the book of Deuteronomy, where more than thirty

times Moses urged his people to deal with their hearts. They were to love God with all their hearts. "Love the LORD your God with all your heart and with all your soul and with all your strength" (6:5). They were to seek Him with all their hearts. "But if from there you seek the LORD your God, you will find him if you look for him with all your heart and with all your soul" (4:29). God's words were to be on their hearts (6:6) and they were to fix His words in their hearts (11:18). He called them to serve Him with all of their hearts (10:12) and with joy and a glad heart (28:47). They were to circumcise their hearts (10:16), that their hearts might not "be led astray" (17:17). Clearly, the heart lies at the core of what it means to know and love God.

Americans tend to think of the heart as the center of emotions. The Bible, however, describes the heart as the meeting place of many different facets of what it means to be human:

- *We think in the heart.* "Knowing their thoughts, Jesus said, 'Why do you entertain evil thoughts in your hearts?' " (Matthew 9:4).

- *We exercise our will in the heart.* "I will harden [Pharaoh's] heart so that he will not let the people go" (Exodus 4:21).

- *The heart trusts in God.* "My heart trusts in him, and I am helped" (Psalm 28:7). *Or they doubt.* "And He said to them, 'Why are you troubled, and why do doubts arise in your hearts?' " (Luke 24:38, NASB).

- *The heart rejoices.* "My heart rejoices in your salvation" (Psalm 13:5). *Or they sorrow.* "How long must I . . . have sorrow in my heart?" (Psalm 13:2).

- *We hate in the heart.* "Do not hate your brother in your heart" (Leviticus 19:17). *We also forgive from the heart.* "This is how my heavenly Father will treat each of you unless you forgive your brother from your heart" (Matthew 18:35).

- It is no wonder, then, that when we sin, that *sin begins in the heart.* "For out of the heart come evil thoughts, murder, adultery, sexual immorality, theft, false testimony, slander" (Matthew 15:19).

Deuteronomy teaches that God wanted the Israelites to serve (*abad*) Him with all of their hearts (i.e., to *do* their acts of worship from the heart). As we can see from above, that would include their thinking, emotions, will, joys, sorrows, fears, hopes, trust and doubts. We have already seen that the Law called them to serve God through sacrifice and offerings. Deuteronomy teaches us that the Israelites could not simply *do* the rituals of sacrifice and offerings unless they did them with all of their hearts.

How would a Hebrew have brought God an offering from the heart? Think of Cain and Abel. They presented God *minhah* offerings. The *minhah* was a way to present oneself to God, asking Him to accept that person as His servant. God accepted Abel and his *minhah*, because in Abel's heart he wanted to belong to God. God rejected Cain and his *minhah,* because in Cain's heart he was only attempting to use the gift as a way to gain God's favor. In his thinking, emotions, will, joys, sorrows, fears, hopes, trust and doubts, Cain did not want to serve God. He simply wanted to use Him.

The controversy at First Community Church probably came from the same attitude. Why did Fred demand that Pastor Rick leave the church? Fred was rejecting the way

Pastor Rick *did* worship (such as singing, raising hands and worship teams), which in biblical terms means the way he *served* (*abad*) the Lord. Perhaps Pastor Rick's *abad* to God was entirely within His revealed will. Perhaps it was not. In order for Fred to serve God with *all of his heart*, he would need to submit his thinking about Rick's worship to the Lord. He would have to say, "Lord, if what Pastor Rick is doing is in Your Word, show me where, so I will change the way I worship." Then when Fred sang to God, his offering would have been *from the heart*. He would have handed over to God what he had naturally thought and taken from God's Word what God wanted him to think. If, however, Fred refused to submit his thinking, which is a part of the heart, to the Lord, his worship would never be from the heart. It would be the same as Cain's worship.

Since *abad* includes both offerings and sacrifice, how did an Israelite bring a sacrifice for sin from the heart? The Hebrew brought his sacrifice with a deep awareness that he had fallen into sin and a deep desire to be restored. This is exactly what David did not do when he committed adultery with Bathsheba and then murdered her husband to hide his sin. He continued to offer sacrifices at the tabernacle for possibly a year after he had committed that atrocity. Every time he brought his offering to the priest at the tabernacle, he would ignore the horror of what he had done. David's attitude was defiant, or "high-handed" (*keyad ramah*). His sacrifice was not from the heart, because he was not submitting his will to God.

Everything changed, however, when Nathan the prophet confronted him. David faced his sin and repented before God. At that point, his attitude toward his sin was no longer *keyad ramah* but contrite and humble. That first sacrifice David brought to God after he confessed his sin must have been a time of profound repentance and relief. For the first time in more than a year, David's sacrifice was from the heart. He wrote Psalm 51 about his experience:

> You do not delight in sacrifice, or I would bring it;
> you do not take pleasure in burnt offerings.
> The sacrifices of God are a broken spirit;
> a broken and contrite heart,
> O God, you will not despise. (Psalm 51:16-17)

Those who present sacrifices with defiant hearts simply refuse to admit their desperate need of cleansing. The Pharisees in the New Testament perfectly illustrate this defiant heart. They continually said in their hearts that they had no sin. Thus, their sacrifices could not cleanse them. Jesus said to them, "If you were blind, you would not be guilty of sin; but now that you claim you can see, your guilt remains" (John 9:41). When the Pharisees brought their offerings to the temple, they were not serving God with all of their hearts, because they did not admit their own sinfulness.

Likewise, when First Community Church sang about the cross of Christ while actively sinning against each other, their *service* of worship had no meaning. Their devotion to the cross hardly could mean much if they hid their sins from the altar, as David hid his sins and the Pharisees hid their sins. The church's dedication to the cross had to come from the heart.

Deuteronomy gives us this most critical principle of worship: Worship without relationship is just ritual. Worship has to come from the heart, and that includes thoughts, will, emotions, hopes, fears, faith, doubts, joys and sorrows. God wanted Israel to serve Him through sacrifice and offering. His highest command was that His worshipers love Him. Therefore, service to God has to be from the heart.

* * *

Continuation of staff meeting, Tuesday morning, February 13

Jeff was the first to break the silence. "Troy," he said, "we are in for a lot of trouble. You know that, don't you?"

Troy nodded his head.

The pastor continued. "We may see this church fall to pieces all around us. It's going to be tough. Are you willing to make that kind of commitment?"

Troy looked at Jeff. "What commitment are you asking me to make?"

Jeff thought for a moment and then turned to the book of Joshua. "Let's take Joshua 24:15 as our promise verse for this coming year: 'But if serving the LORD seems undesirable to you, then choose for yourselves this day whom you will serve, whether the gods your forefathers served beyond the River, or the gods of the Amorites, in whose land you are living. But as for me and my household, we will serve the LORD.' "

QUESTION:
According to Moses, what did God
require of Israel for worship?

PRINCIPLE 5:

B: According to Moses, God required Israel to serve Him with all of their hearts through offerings and sacrifice.

What the Law Taught about Music in Worship

Choir practice, Wednesday evening, February 14

There was an uncomfortable feeling running through the choir room. Usually choir members were busy chatting and arranging their music folders. This evening, however, they were quiet. Everyone was wondering why the pastor was sitting up front. Troy looked out over the group and wondered how they would respond to the new plan.

"All right, everybody, let's get started." Troy took his position at the podium and waited for the final stragglers to sit down. He looked over the seats and saw three empty— Fred's, Janice's (Fred's wife) and Rebecca's.

They opened in prayer.

Troy swallowed hard and braced himself. "OK, to start things off, I have three announcements. Starting this Saturday evening, at 7:00 at my house, we'll be having a choir prayer time. I really need all of you to come. Second, we are going to take the next three months off as a choir. We won't be singing in the services again until June. Third, as of this Sunday, the pastor and I have decided that we are stopping all music for our worship services too, probably for three months as well. " Troy looked over at Jeff, sitting in the front row. "Pastor, do you have anything to add to that?"

Pastor Jeff stood and faced the choir. "Not really, Troy. I figured that you all are going to have lots of questions, so here I am. Would anybody like to ask anything?"

Donna raised her hand. "Pastor, do you mean we won't be doing hymns or choruses for three whole months?"

Jeff nodded. "No singing at all."

Donna frowned. "What about the piano and organ?"

Pastor Jeff looked over at Troy, standing next to him. Troy answered. "We've told Darlene and Lois that we're not going to use them at the piano and organ for the next three months. When we explained why, they both agreed."

While Troy spoke, the pastor was watching Tom. The plan clearly was upsetting him. Jeff decided to give him a chance to speak. "Tom, how do you feel about this?"

Overflowing with anger, Tom burst out, "How in the world are we going to attract the unsaved to our church if we don't have music? Nobody's going to want to come to First Community without music!"

Troy saw many heads nodding in the choir room.

Charles spoke up. "Pastor, how can we do worship as a church without singing? Worship in the Old Testament always came with singing. Music is the foundation of worship in the Bible!"

Charles' passion worried Pastor Jeff. He knew that their decision might make some people very unhappy, and Charles was one of them. He carefully answered. "I thought so, until I started studying it. In the Bible, music is not always as important to worship as we might think."

Troy knew that Charles would never accept that, so he began praying fervently that God would defuse the tension before they had a serious confrontation.

Charles shrugged. "All I know is that the largest book of the Bible is dedicated to worship music. You can say what you want, Pastor. Music goes to the heart of worship."

*   *   *

Whether or not Jeff's idea was a good one, the choir's reaction should not have surprised him. Imagining corporate worship without music is hard for most Christians. Yet studying the Law of Moses would surprise

most of them, for God did not direct Moses to incorporate music into Israel's worship.

We can guess that the children of Israel loved music.
Moses tells us of two occasions when the Hebrews sang
to the Lord in a spontaneous outburst of praise and
thanksgiving. The first was after God led them through
the Red Sea. "Then Moses and the Israelites sang this
song to the LORD: 'I will sing to the LORD, for he is highly
exalted. The horse and its rider he has hurled into the
sea' " (Exodus 15:1). The women responded with joy.
"Then Miriam the prophetess, Aaron's sister, took a tam-
bourine in her hand, and all the women followed her,
with tambourines and dancing. Miriam sang to them:
'Sing to the LORD, for he is highly exalted. The horse and
its rider he has hurled into the sea' " (15:20-21).

The Torah records one other time that the Hebrews
sang out in spontaneous praise. During their wilderness
journey, they had bitterly rebelled against God when
drinkable water was scarce (Exodus 15:23-24). In Numbers 21, they burst into song when the Lord promised
them water.

> From there they continued on to Beer, the well
> where the LORD said to Moses, "Gather the people
> together and I will give them water." Then Israel
> sang this song: "Spring up, O well! Sing about it,
> about the well that the princes dug, that the nobles
> of the people sank—the nobles with scepters and
> staffs." (Numbers 21:16-18)

Other than these two instances, the first five books of
the Old Testament do not describe the Israelites singing.

What kind of music did the Hebrews sing? Most likely,
they sang music that flowed from their culture. They

surely sang celebration songs at times of great joy. Songs of mourning probably accompanied times of great sorrow. We can guess that music was a very important part of their lives. That makes us wonder why God did not make music a part of Israel's formal worship.

The Law of Moses carefully laid out many commandments for Israel's worship. The Law describes the sacrifices, temple, priestly garments, anointing oils, feasts and other aspects of worship. For that matter, the Law carefully regulates food, dress, marriage, family, civil relationships and a myriad of other everyday issues. Yet for some reason, the Law of Moses entirely ignores teaching the Israelites what they were supposed to do with music in their *abad*, their service of worship to the Lord.

Perhaps God did not include music in the Law of Moses because Israel's culture was still too Egyptian. Perhaps their music itself was too Egyptian, and using it in worship might cause them to see worship the way Egyptian idolaters saw it. We can speculate as to the reason, but the Bible does not mention why music was omitted from the Law. (In chapter 6, we will look at how, centuries later, David finally brought music into Israel's worship.)

If the people at First Community Church had searched the Law for a solution to their dilemma, they would have been disappointed. They would not have found anything about worship there. If they had considered this strange silence, they might have realized that music was not as important to Moses as it was to them. The fact that God did not incorporate music into Israel's worship suggests that music is not essential to worship. Perhaps that realization might have helped them to be less intent on finding the right music style and more intent on serving God from the heart.

For hundreds of years, when the Israelites worshiped they simply presented their offerings and sacrifices without the accompaniment of music. Surely those bloody sacrifices stirred the emotions of those who truly felt the weight of their sins. Music would have aided them in that, but God withheld that aid. Perhaps the most likely reason centered on the sacrifices and offerings themselves. Without music, the sinner's repentance as he offered sacrifice and the innocent victim's suffering provided all the meaning to worship. That was all that was necessary to come to God and worship Him.

*   *   *

Continuation of choir practice, Wednesday evening, February 14

Janice raised her hand. "Pastor, what are we going to do during the worship service if we don't have music?"

Pastor Jeff smiled. "Well, Troy and I are working on that. We'll certainly go through some Psalms. We'd like some suggestions from all of you."

The room was silent. Troy waited for a long and awkward minute before saying anything. "Our real goal for the worship service is that we learn to refocus our eyes back on Christ. We need to see the cross again. So if any of you can suggest how to do that, I would really appreciate it."

Nobody seemed terribly eager to volunteer any ideas, so Jeff closed the meeting in prayer. As people began to leave, Troy wondered what people were thinking. He looked over at his pastor, who was talking in the corner with one of the deacons, and prayed silently. *How long, Lord, will this go on before we see a breakthrough? How long will this church stay together?*

Q U E S T I O N :
According to Moses, how did music
relate to Israel's worship?

P R I N C I P L E 5 :

C: God did not reveal to Moses what part music
was to play in Israel's worship.

Worship: God Required Israel to Remember

Staff meeting, Thursday afternoon, February 15

Pastor Jeff looked over at Troy, sitting across from his desk. His worship pastor was deep in thought.

They had made great progress already that morning, having agreed upon how they would plan Sunday services. First, every week Jeff and Troy would spend Tuesday morning together in prayer. They would ask a simple question of God: "What do You want us to do this Sunday morning?" When they came to a clear answer, they would make that their prayer goal for the week. The prayer goal had to center on each believer's personal relationship with Christ. Then, they would focus their prayer throughout the week on that goal. For this coming Sunday, Troy and Jeff were praying that God would help each believer to apply Christ's cross to their own hearts. The two pastors were asking God to help their congregation believe in His love for them so that they would truly trust Him.

Second, they agreed that Troy would come up with a list of different approaches to the Sunday morning service. Each part of the service had to help church members grow in relationship to the overall prayer goal. This first Sunday was focusing on the cross. Troy and Jeff had specific goals for each segment of the service, all based upon their overall goal. They were praying that the Scripture readings would help remind the church of the terrible price Christ paid on the cross. They were hoping that the testimonies would reveal how Christ's cross had actually changed the lives of their fellow members. They included an extended time of prayer with the goal that each person there would pray for others to grow in understanding the cross in their own lives. Jeff already decided that if Troy could not figure out what to pray about for an aspect of the service, it did not need to be in the service.

Third, on Friday both pastors would again set aside all morning for prayer together. They would pray about every part of the service, for each prayer goal and for their overall prayer goal. They would pray that God would accomplish His work in the lives of specific individuals through the service. Then they would pray for each other as well.

Fourth, Troy would lead the choir prayer meeting Saturday evenings. Jeff wanted that time to be where choir members began to catch a vision for what God wanted to accomplish. Of course, it would work only if choir members showed up. This Saturday evening, they would pray about remembering the cross.

Jeff smiled. Only a miracle could make this happen. If God was in this, First Community Church was in for growth like it had never known.

*   *   *

Jeff and Troy struggled to find a way to help the congregation remember Christ's cross. Because their church was typical of many Christian churches, the cross at times was nothing more than a token, a piece of jewelry or a sentimental symbol. Teaching people to look again at Christ's cross would be no easy task, because the congregation had grown comfortably familiar with it.

Why is remembering so important in the Bible? The answer is simple: Biblical religion is founded upon history. The prophets foretold Christ's coming. Christ came, taught and healed. Real sinners with real names crucified Christ on a real cross in a real city on a real date in history. Jesus broke the bonds of death on the Sunday after that historical date. Also, we are commanded to remember the glorious things that God has done in Christ. "He took bread, gave thanks and broke it, and gave it to them, saying, 'This is my body given for you; do this in remembrance of me' " (Luke 22:19). "Remember Jesus Christ, raised from the dead, descended from David. This is my gospel" (2 Timothy 2:8). "What, then, shall we say in response to this? If God is for us, who can be against us? He who did not spare his own Son, but gave him up for us all—how will he not also, along with him, graciously give us all things?" (Romans 8:31-32). The New Testament writers encourage us to grow in Christ by reminding us of what God did for us through Christ's cross.

God commanded Israel throughout its history to look back on the past and remember. When He prepared the children of Israel to escape from Egypt, He commanded Moses to teach them that in the future they were to remember what He was about to do. God created a holy week (the Passover and Feast of Unleavened Bread) so that the Israelites would remember what He had done for them. "This is a day you are to commemorate; for the generations to come you shall celebrate it as a festival to the LORD—a lasting ordinance" (Exodus 12:14). God designed Passover and the Feast of Unleavened Bread as tools to help them remember His work among them in the past.

Think of all the petty jealousies that divided the disciples the night Jesus was betrayed. "Also a dispute arose among them as to which of them was considered to be greatest" (Luke 22:24). Yet if any of them had stood on Calvary that next day, who would have bragged while watching his Lord and Master dying on the cross? At the foot of the cross, their differences would not have seemed important.

Could it be that the people of First Community Church needed to go "out there" to the cross and stand in its shadow? Could it be that these Christians were fighting among themselves because they had forgotten the cross, the pain, the suffering and the sacrifice of the Savior, for whom they were named?

In the Law, God made these times of remembering—Passover and the Feast of Unleavened Bread—significant pilgrimage feasts (*chagag*). Once Solomon built the temple, Jews from all over the world made their way to Jerusalem in celebration of Passover. Meaning overflowed during the days of Passover and the Feast of Unleavened Bread. This was true for all of Israel's feasts. These were not boring or formulaic rituals, but celebrations rich in visual imagery. To help Israel remember well, God used all the senses—touch, taste, smell, sight and sound. For example, to commemorate their time in the wilderness, God commanded Israel to construct booths and live in them for one week, which must have been a very holistic experience (Leviticus 23:42-43).

Deuteronomy 26:2-4 describes the Feast of Firstfruits (later called Pentecost) as a profoundly hands-on experience. God commanded them:

> Take some of the firstfruits of all that you produce from the soil of the land the LORD your God is giving you and put them in a basket. Then go to the place the LORD your God will choose as a dwelling for his Name and say to the priest in office at the time, "I declare today to the LORD your God that I have come to the land the LORD swore to our forefathers to give us." The priest shall take the basket from your hands and set it down in front of the altar of the LORD your God.

Of course, at Passover the Hebrew carried his lamb, slaughtered it, personally took its blood and applied it to the lintels of his house, cooked the lamb and ate it, all the while reciting the wonders God performed in rescuing Israel from Pharaoh's clutches. All of these experiences caused the Jews to relive what their forefathers had experienced long ago.

Israel worshiped by serving God with offerings and sacrifices. The Israelites also worshiped by placing themselves in proper relationship to the Lord of the universe. And God commanded His people to worship Him by remembering (i.e., by celebrating feasts designed to help them remember God's acts of mercy and power in the past).

If the people of First Community Church were to overcome their division, they would have to return to the foot of the cross. God forged the only unity they could know through the crucifixion of His Son, Jesus Christ.

>   For he himself is our peace, who has made the two
>   one and has destroyed the barrier, the dividing wall
>   of hostility, by abolishing in his flesh the law with its
>   commandments and regulations. His purpose was to
>   create in himself one new man out of the two, thus
>   making peace, and in this one body to reconcile both
>   of them to God through the cross, by which he put to
>   death their hostility. (Ephesians 2:14-16)

First Community Church had to force itself to gaze again upon the crown of thorns. First Community Church needed to hear Jesus speak these words again: "Father, forgive them, for they do not know what they are doing" (Luke 23:34).

*   *   *

Troy looked up at Jeff. "You know, Jeff, it's going to be hard to find ways to help our people remember Christ's cross. We all take it for granted. But nothing is more important. Paul said, 'We preach Christ crucified: a stumbling block to Jews and foolishness to Gentiles, but to those whom God has called, both Jews and Greeks, Christ the power of God and the wisdom of God' (1 Corinthians 1:23-24). God has to help us see the cross for what it really is."

Picking up a Bible, Jeff flipped to the passage in First Corinthians and thoughtfully read it. Troy watched as he kept reading silently. "Troy, listen to this," he finally said. " 'For I resolved to know nothing while I was with you except Jesus Christ and him crucified' " (2:2).

He placed the Bible on his desk and looked up at his worship pastor. "When you and I have this kind of ministry," he said, "if we determine to know nothing with our people except Jesus Christ and Him crucified, then they'll follow."

Troy nodded. "I guess, then, that's our job. Make Jesus Christ and His cross the center of our worship time again."

QUESTION:
According to Moses, what else did God
require of Israel for worship?

PRINCIPLE 5:

D: According to Moses, God required Israel to worship Him by remembering His mighty saving acts.

FIVE

What Makes My Worship Holy?

QUESTION:
What makes my worship holy?

PRINCIPLE 6:

My worship is holy only if what I bring God is wholly His.

QUESTION:
How can I tell if I am committing idolatry?

PRINCIPLE 7:

A: I am committing idolatry when I change God to make Him easier to understand and approach.

B: I am committing idolatry when I seek to bypass my relationship with God in order to gain whatever I desire.

Choir prayer meeting, Saturday evening, February 17

Troy nervously looked over at Isabelle, who was calmly sitting on their living room couch. "Well, it's 6:55 and nobody has shown up yet. Looks like our idea of a choir prayer meeting didn't quite catch on."

Isabelle smiled. "Troy, I almost think that you would be happier if nobody showed up at all. It's not supposed to start until 7:00 anyway."

Suddenly the doorbell rang. Isabelle opened the door to Mindy and Marcia. Pretty soon Oliver and his wife, Andrea, joined them.

Six people total. *Funny,* Troy thought, *the people who showed up aren't really on either side of the worship war.* Six people praying seemed like a small group to tackle such a big problem. Well, they would have to be like David against Goliath, small in the sight of the world, but trusting in a great God.

Troy began. "Tonight I would like us to pray mostly for the choir itself. Ever since I got here, I've felt like the choir is the key to healing our church."

Oliver shook his head. "Troy, the choir is more divided than even the church."

"I know," the worship minister sighed. "We simply have to change how we view ourselves. I almost feel as if both sides see the church's worship ministry as their own private property. One side says, 'We know that our worship is the right worship.' The other side says, 'This is our church and we don't want anyone to change the way our church worships.' "

Mindy broke in. "That's horrible! Nobody owns First Community Church. I mean, only God owns this church."

Troy nodded in agreement. "That's how I feel about the choir too. Do we all agree that it isn't our choir, but God's choir?" The small group nodded. "Then we have no business using the choir to please ourselves. This choir belongs to God."

Isabelle reminded them, "Then God needs to teach us how to give the choir back to Him. Let's pray."

An hour later, Isabelle shut the door as the last car pulled away. She leaned her head against the door. *Father,* she prayed silently, *it's all up to You now. Please make this choir solely and completely Yours. Make us holy, Lord.*

* * *

Holy Worship from a Holy People

Isabelle prayed that God would make the people at First Community Church holy. But what does it mean for a church to be holy? Many Christians treat holiness as if it were a special power, a mystical presence of God. They talk about "holy places" and "holy icons." If we want to understand the real nature of holiness, we must study what the Old Testament says about it.

The word translated "holy" (Hebrew *qodesh* or *qadosh*) occurs more than 200 times in Exodus, Leviticus, Numbers and Deuteronomy. A related word, often translated as "sanctify" (Hebrew *qadash*, which is the verb "to make holy") occurs some sixty times.

In the Law of Moses, the word *holy* occasionally refers to God Himself. "I am the LORD your God; consecrate yourselves and be holy, because I am holy" (Leviticus 11:44). Often *holy* refers to various aspects of life in Israel. For example, an Israelite could make a holy vow, as in Leviticus 27. Whatever the Israelite vowed to the Lord was considered holy, so that it then belonged to God and was His alone. The Israelite had to redeem or surrender that holy thing, whether animal, land or tithe (Leviticus 27:1-10).

When the Bible describes things as holy, it means that they were devoted to God as His personal possession. "But nothing that a man owns and devotes to the LORD—whether man or animal or family land—may be sold or redeemed; everything so devoted is most holy to the LORD" (27:28). The holy things in the Old Testament had nothing sacred or mysterious about them in any way. They simply had become God's possession. That is what *holy* means in the Old Testament.

Most of the time the word *holy* appears, it has some reference to the tabernacle or the general worship of Israel. It refers to parts of the tabernacle and especially the holy of holies (some versions correctly translate this as "the most holy place"). In addition, the priests wore holy garments (Exodus 28:2). The flesh of the sacrifice was holy (Exodus 29:33), as were the firstborn offerings (Leviticus 27:26-28). The Israelites were to view these things as God's possessions and therefore holy.

When Isabelle prayed that God would make the choir holy, she meant exactly this. The music they sang on Sunday mornings needed to belong to God. The different factions had no right to demand that the Sunday morning worship should conform to their personal preferences. Fred had tried to win Troy over to his way of "doing worship." In reality, he was attempting to take possession of something that belonged solely to God. By definition, if Fred had succeeded, whatever First Community Church would have done for morning worship would not have been holy at all, because it would not have belonged to God. We cannot hold on to those things we devote to the Lord. We must let go of them as our possessions and give them completely over to God to use however He chooses. That is what makes worship holy.

In the Law, the Israelites themselves were also holy people. They were a holy assembly (Exodus 12:16). " 'Now if you obey me fully and keep my covenant, then out of all nations you will be my treasured possession. Although the whole earth is mine, you will be for me a kingdom of priests and a holy nation.' These are the words you are to speak to the Israelites" (19:5-6). Notice that God calls them His "treasured possession." God owned Israel; therefore, His people were holy. Whatever belongs to God as His possession is holy.

Because the Israelites were holy, they were to separate themselves from the way the rest of the nations lived. For example, they were to be careful what they ate. "You are to be my holy people. So do not eat the meat of an animal torn by wild beasts; throw it to the dogs" (22:31). God dictated many other details in their lives to remind the Hebrews that He had set them apart solely for Himself.

Ten times God declared Himself to be their Sanctifier, which is another word for "make holy." "Say to the Israelites, 'You must observe my Sabbaths. This will be a sign between me and you for the generations to come, so you may know that I am the LORD, who makes you holy' " (31:13). The fact that God was their Sanctifier was a reason for them to walk in holiness. "Keep my decrees and follow them. I am the LORD, who makes you holy" (Leviticus 20:8). Because God is holy, they were to be holy too. "I am the LORD who brought you up out of Egypt to be your God; therefore be holy, because I am holy" (Leviticus 11:45).

When Isabelle prayed that God would make the choir holy, she was handing over possession of their music to the Lord. She also was asking Him to take the choir members themselves. They were supposed to be God's own possessions. "Do you not know that your body is a temple of the Holy Spirit, who is in you, whom you have received from God? You are not your own" (1 Corinthians 6:19). People are holy only when they give up their self-possession and surrender their rights to God. Sanctification, which means "the work of making something holy," begins when believers give up their personal rights for control. They transfer ownership rights completely over to Jesus Christ and ask Him to direct their hopes and desires.

There is no place for bickering and fighting among those who worship. Their worship is supposed to be holy, belonging to God alone. All worshipers are supposed to be holy, God's possessions. They have no rights. They have no privileges. They have no personal preferences. They and their worship is holy.

In the Law, time itself could be holy, such as holy convocations. "Speak to the Israelites and say to them: 'These are my appointed feasts, the appointed feasts of the LORD, which you are to proclaim as sacred assemblies' " (Leviticus 23:2). On holy convocations or assemblies, God did not permit the Israelites to work. Instead, they were to come together to celebrate. "On the fifteenth day of the seventh month, hold a sacred assembly

and do no regular work. Celebrate a festival to the LORD
for seven days" (Numbers 29:12). Do not think that holy
time had some mystical power or sacredness about it.
There is not one phrase, verse, paragraph, chapter or
book of the Old Testament that hints God was present
among the Israelites on holy days in a special way. The
days were holy because they belonged to God as His own
possession. Because God owned those days, the Israelites
had no right to use them for their purposes.

The Sabbath also was a holy time in Israel. The Ten
Commandments required that Israel set apart the Sabbath as a sacred day. "Remember the Sabbath day by
keeping it holy" (Exodus 20:8). Apparently, the heart of
keeping the Sabbath holy was to abstain from all work.

> Observe the Sabbath, because it is holy to you.
> Anyone who desecrates it must be put to death; who-
> ever does any work on that day must be cut off from
> his people. For six days, work is to be done, but the
> seventh day is a Sabbath of rest, holy to the LORD.
> Whoever does any work on the Sabbath day must be
> put to death. (31:14-15)

Because God owned the Sabbath, the Hebrews could
not use that day for their purposes.

When Isabelle prayed that God would make the choir
holy, she also was praying that their time together, in
practice, in prayer and in ministry, would belong to God
alone. When the choir came together, their time was not
theirs to do as they pleased. Their personal pleasures and
desires were not relevant. God owned that choir practice.
God owned that prayer meeting. God owned that worship service. That time was holy.

God owned the tabernacle (and later its replacement, the temple) as His own possession, His dwelling place on earth. God took His possession, His dwelling place, and placed it among the Israelites, even though they were sinful. "You must keep the Israelites separate from things that make them unclean, so they will not die in their uncleanness for defiling my dwelling place, which is among them" (Leviticus 15:31). The tabernacle made Israel holy because God dwelled within it. In addition, God's holy presence in the tabernacle exposed and revealed their wickedness, and thus condemned them. That's why the Israelites had to sanctify (make holy) themselves by bringing sacrifices to the tabernacle.

Because the tabernacle (later the temple) was God's dwelling place on earth, the Law required that Israel bring to that place alone all of its formal worship—sacrifices and offerings. Remember that to a Hebrew, real worship was all about presenting God with sacrifices and offerings. The Old Testament's historical books indicate that worship almost always happened at the tabernacle. The tabernacle was the only place on earth where humankind could legitimately bring sacrifices to God. Israel was a nation of priests to the world. The tabernacle was God's dwelling where the world met God.

Holy worship meant something very specific to the Hebrew. Worshipers had to cleanse themselves of sin through sincere sacrifices. They had to bring to God offerings that belonged wholly to the Lord. And everything God set apart as His own possession, whether time (the Sabbath), place (the temple) or object (something devoted to God), had to belong to Him alone.

This surely is the background of Romans 12:1: "There-fore, I urge you, brothers, in view of God's mercy, to of-fer your bodies as living sacrifices, holy and pleasing to God—this is your spiritual act of worship." This also must be the background of First Timothy 2:8: "I want men everywhere to lift up holy hands in prayer, with-out anger or disputing." A holy sacrifice is one that be-longs to God alone. Holy hands are hands that have not been defiled by anger and disputing. Holy worship is worship that belongs solely to the Lord.

*   *   *

Isabelle sat down next to her tired husband on the couch. Troy looked discouraged. She worried that the strain at church was beginning to wear him down.

He looked up at her. "You know, Isabelle, this church doesn't belong to us."

Isabelle nodded her head.

"I'm the choir director, but God owns the choir too."

Isabelle agreed quietly, "I know, Troy."

Troy looked into Isabelle's eyes. "I'm having a hard time allowing God to do whatever He wants to do with His church. He might 'mess things up' for us. He might take ev-erything I want and throw it away and do something com-pletely different."

Troy reached over and took the hand of his wife of ten years. "But I want this choir to belong to Jesus and Jesus alone. Not to me, not to you, not to Pastor Jeff."

Isabelle nodded in agreement. "Troy, it's time we get out of the way. Let's dedicate the choir and the church to the Lord. Let's give it to Him and let Him do with it whatever He pleases."

QUESTION:
What makes my worship holy?

PRINCIPLE 6:

My worship is holy only if what I bring God is
wholly His.

Holy People Who Worship God and God Alone

Charles and Sharlene's home, Tuesday evening, February 27

Charles continued the argument they had begun on the
way home from church on Sunday. "I can't go to a dead
church service week after week. There's just no point."

Sharlene quietly replied, "I don't agree, Charles. Something good is happening at our church. We need to stay."

Her husband shook his head. "Sharlene, nothing has
been happening in months. Where's the victory at First
Community Church? We are children of the King of kings!
We're supposed to be celebrating Jesus, overflowing with
joy! There's no joy at First Community Church. There's no
blessing. It's dead."

Three years ago, Sharlene would have agreed with her
husband. That was before their son, Chris, had been diag-
nosed with Pompe Disease (Acid Maltase Deficiency), a
rare and always fatal form of muscular dystrophy. She had
taken Chris to every healing service, but to no avail. The

preachers all promised happiness and joy. Sharlene, however, knew no happiness as she watched her son's strength
slowly fail. But she did find joy. During his last agonizing
days, Chris showed Sharlene a kind of joy she had never
known. In the midst of his profound suffering, Chris continually assured her, "Don't worry, Mom. It won't hurt much
longer. I'm going to be with Jesus." Chris was not happy, but
he knew joy.

After Chris died, Sharlene went through profound grief,
hour after hour, day after day. In the throes of her agony,
Chris' words came to her over and over again. "Don't
worry, Mom. It won't hurt much longer. I'm going to be
with Jesus." Sharlene began to find the same joy Chris had
shown during his hardest days. The joy was not a feeling and
it was not a power that made the sorrow light. Strangely, the
joy made itself most clearly known in the darkest hours of
her heartache. It was an assurance that Jesus was in control,
that He was entirely and always good, that He knew her
pain and shared it, and that He loved Chris more than she
could ever have loved him. It was a certainty that, no matter
what, she and Charles were going to be with Chris forever
and ever in the presence of Jesus.

That is why Sharlene finally told Charles that Tuesday
evening what she had wanted to say for months. "Charles,
you are not looking for joy in Jesus. You are looking for a
feeling of happiness. You want sweetness and painlessness
and blissfulness. But that's not blessing, Charles. That's not
joy."

He looked at his wife in shock.

She continued. "You talk so much about blessing. You
want the service to bless you. You want to be filled with joy.
What if something comes along that isn't bright and cheer-

ful? To you it isn't a blessing. If it isn't bright and cheerful, you don't see the joy in it."

Charles opened his mouth to protest, but found no words.

Sharlene laid her hand upon her husband's hand and continued. "I can't live that way, Charles." Her eyes began to fill with tears. "I want the real God. The One who chose to call Chris home to Himself. The One who led us through all of this pain."

Tears were now flowing down her face. "Chris' death was too painful for me to try to turn Jesus into some kind of happy God who is always smiling. That's a false idol. I want to face Him the way He really is."

Charles stopped trying to argue with her. He was just trying to understand what she was saying.

Sharlene squeezed her husband's hand. "Don't cut out the passages in the Bible that talk about God bringing pain to our lives, Charles. If you do that, you'll be creating a new God and a new religion. All of your songs about joy and happiness and victory are just too one-sided. God brings blessing through the cross, not through singing and clapping."

She paused for a moment and picked up her Bible. "Here are the blessings Jesus promised. 'Blessed are the poor in spirit, for theirs is the kingdom of heaven. Blessed are those who mourn, for they will be comforted' " (Matthew 5:3-4).

Sharlene looked into her husband's eyes. She could see that he was listening. "That's why I don't want to leave our church right now. I want to worship the true God, the God whose joy often comes in the form of pain. That's why I don't think we need music at First Community Church right now in order to worship God. Do you understand?"

*   *   *

Sharlene and Charles were wrestling with a problem that all Christians encounter: How can a loving God allow good people to suffer? Sharlene knew that the Bible teaches that God often brings suffering into the lives of those whom He loves. Charles, on the other hand, denied that God would ever do that. Charles saw his son's illness as Satan's attack. He secretly blamed himself for not having enough faith to rebuke the illness and believe God for healing. (Note: Several times in the past few years I have heard people express exactly that guilt: "I just didn't have enough faith.") Even though so many Scripture passages describe God as bringing pain into our lives (see, for example, Hebrews 12:4-13; Matthew 10:38-39; and 2 Corinthians 4-5), Charles could not relate to a God who leads His children into pain and suffering. Therefore, he subconsciously changed what God is like so that he could relate to Him more easily. When Charles made God easier to understand, he was committing a form of idolatry.

When was the last time you heard a sermon that even mentioned the word *idolatry*? How can Christians today recognize what idolatry looks like in a post-Christian world?

One of the clearest examples of idolatry happened when the sons of Israel created the idol of a golden calf and worshiped it as the Lord. Idolatry comes in two different forms. Either one creates a false idol of the true God, or one creates an idol of a false god. That day on the plain before Mount Sinai, the Israelites committed the first kind of idolatry. They created a false image of the Lord and worshiped it.

The first kind of idolatry: creating a different God and calling it the Lord. After God led the children of Israel across the

Red Sea, He called Moses to climb Mount Sinai and meet with Him. Moses was gone for forty days and the people began to worry. They had grown up with idolatry during their years in Egypt, so their natural reaction was to turn back to worshiping idols. "When the people saw that Moses was so long in coming down from the mountain, they gathered around Aaron and said, 'Come, make us gods who will go before us. As for this fellow Moses who brought us up out of Egypt, we don't know what has happened to him' " (Exodus 32:1).

Thus, Aaron formed an idol so that the people could have something tangible to worship. "He took what they handed him and made it into an idol cast in the shape of a calf, fashioning it with a tool. Then they said, 'These are your gods, O Israel, who brought you up out of Egypt' " (32:4). Here is the key to understanding this kind of idolatry: They called the golden calf the "gods . . . who brought you up out of Egypt."

Aaron understood exactly what the people meant. "When Aaron saw this, he built an altar in front of the calf and announced, 'Tomorrow there will be a festival to the LORD' " (32:5). Notice that Aaron dedicated the feast to the LORD. The Hebrew word for "LORD" is Yahweh, which is God's personal name. Aaron assumed that he had fashioned an idol of Yahweh, the Lord of the universe. Aaron did not think for a moment that Yahweh, the LORD, existed in the shape of a calf. He simply thought that the golden calf would attract Yahweh's presence, so that His power would dwell there.

God had warned Israel not to make any idols. "You shall not make for yourself an idol in the form of anything in heaven above or on the earth beneath or in the waters below. You shall not bow down to them or worship them" (20:4-5). The people knew that God's name meant that He is who He is and they had no right to try to make Him something else. "God said to Moses, 'I AM WHO I AM. This is what you are to say to the Israelites: "I AM has sent me to you" ' " (3:14).

When life became difficult for the people of Israel, however, they did not comprehend how a God whom they could not see nor understand would help them. They wanted to change Him so that He would be more accessible to them, more familiar to them, easier to grasp. So they transformed God from "I AM WHO I AM" to a golden calf. They could understand that. They had grown up in a world of false gods whose "power" dwelled in statues just like this one. Now they could see the "Lord" who had delivered them from Pharaoh.

Yahweh, the LORD, however, had not changed from "I AM WHO I AM" to a golden statue. He was still invisible, infinite. No man could fashion a statue to draw His mighty presence. We cannot change the Lord into something easy to understand, something readily available, something smooth to the touch. He always remains, "I AM WHO I AM."

Life became difficult for Charles and Sharlene when their son, Chris, was dying. They responded in two ways. Sharlene bowed before the unseen Lord and sought to understand Him by studying and believing His words in the Bible. She discovered that His joy is not easy to grasp, but often filled with pain. She found the Apostle Paul's teaching that fulfillment comes in the Christian life "known, yet regarded as unknown; dying, and yet we live on; beaten, and yet not killed; sorrowful, yet always rejoicing; poor, yet making many rich; having nothing, and yet possessing everything" (2 Corinthians 6:9-10). Sharlene came to God as "I AM WHO I AM." She refused to change Him to fit her meager understanding of life and reality. Instead, she adjusted what she grasped about life to fit what God had already revealed about Himself in His Word.

Charles, on the other hand, changed what God was like. God was no longer "I AM WHO I AM" for Charles, but became "I AM WHOM YOU CAN UNDERSTAND." Charles could understand a God of power and glory and happiness and victory. So he ignored the biblical passages that focus on the other side of God, the side of the cross. Charles assumed that blessings are always bright, that joy is always happy. He refused to believe that victory often comes in the form of a cross. He created a different god and called him the Lord, because he could not understand the God of the Bible, who brings us sorrowful joys and painful blessings. Charles committed a form of idolatry.

Worshiping an idol is sin because idolatry undermines the relationship between the worshiper and God just as surely as a lie undermines trust. God created us so that He could take hidden treasures within Himself and share those treasures with us. Idolatry mocks that relationship. When we change God to fit our paltry minds and experiences, we lose the wonder and the joy of knowing Him the way He really is. Our false gods cannot speak and cannot act. "Like a scarecrow in a melon patch, their idols cannot speak; they must be carried because they cannot walk. Do not fear them;

they can do no harm nor can they do any good" (Jeremiah 10:5). How is fellowship with God possible when we transform Him into another god, a dumb idol?

Often people commit idolatry today the way the Hebrews did with the calf. They are not looking for another god. They are simply looking for a way to make God easier to access. They still call their man-made creation "God." They say to Him, "Worshiping You is now so much easier, Lord. Now I can understand You."

Why do people commit this kind of idolatry? They generally create idols to get something from the Divine. They suppose that idols are like a television antenna that concentrates God's divine power and presence into the statue or location. By going to an idol, they bypass a relationship with God. All they need are the right mystical words, sacred rituals and spiritual intensity, and they'll get whatever they want.

When we have a relationship with God, we must take His Word and deal with it honestly within ourselves. Sometimes that is very unpleasant. God answers us according to His best plans for us, but we may not like His plans. Idols, on the other hand, have no plans—just power. Paul said that even though idols are nothing, we must remember that demons use our attraction to images to ensnare us. "Do I mean then that a sacrifice offered to an idol is anything, or that an idol is anything? No, but the sacrifices of pagans are offered to demons, not to God, and I do not want you to be participants with demons" (1 Corinthians 10:19-20). When people trust in idols, without even realizing it, they are actually trusting in demons.

When God responds to our prayers, He works to build up our relationship with Him. When an idol seems to respond, from the idolater's viewpoint it is because he has used the right words and rituals to release its concentration of divine presence and power. In reality, it may well be because the demons are simply using the idolater's naïveté to ensnare him.

The God of the Bible gives only those gifts that are good. "Every good and perfect gift is from above, coming down from the Father of the heavenly lights, who does not change like shifting shadows" (James 1:17). Sometimes those good gifts come in the form of suffering. "Consider it pure joy, my brothers, whenever you face trials of many kinds, because you know that the testing of your faith develops perseverance" (1:2-3). Idols, however, do not even know what good is. People who commit idolatry, who fashion false gods, do not want a relationship; they want results.

QUESTION:
How can I tell if I am committing idolatry?

PRINCIPLE 7:

A: I am committing idolatry when I change God to make Him easier to understand and approach.

The second kind of idolatry: adopting new gods alongside the Lord. There is a second kind of idolatry, which is more visible than the first. People adopt other gods, usually (but not always) from other religions. In the Old Testament, many times Israel turned to worship foreign gods.

The people often continued to "worship" the Lord while pursuing Baal or Molech. Not too many Christians fall into that kind of idolatry directly, but this second kind of idolatry has a subtle variation: greed.

Paul said that a covetous man is an idolater. "For of this you can be sure: No immoral, impure or greedy person—such a man is an idolater—has any inheritance in the kingdom of Christ and of God" (Ephesians 5:5). People who desire money want to bypass trusting in God so that they can have whatever they want. Suppose I want a new car. If I have no money, the only way I can get a car is if God provides it. What if God does not want me to have a new car? Then because I have no money, I will not get one. If, however, I have the money, then even if God did not want me to have the car I could still buy it myself.

What stands in the way of my having a new car? My lack of money, or God? The correct answer depends on who my god really is. If the Lord of the universe is my God, then He is the one standing in the way of my having a new car. I will have to work out what He wants for me through our relationship together. If money is my god, then my lack of wealth blocks the way to my new car. I do not care what God wants for me, but only what will satisfy my desires. I am being greedy and that makes me an idolater. "Put to death, therefore, whatever belongs to your earthly nature: sexual immorality, impurity, lust, evil desires and greed, which is idolatry" (Colossians 3:5). American Christians do not even seem to fight against this second kind of idolatry. We have brought the false gods of money and security alongside the Lord. We worship God on Sunday morning and money the rest of the week.

All throughout the Bible, God says that He is a jealous God. We cannot love God and love the world at the same time.

> You adulteresses, do you not know that friendship with the world is hostility toward God? Therefore whoever wishes to be a friend of the world makes himself an enemy of God. Or do you think that the Scripture speaks to no purpose: "He jealously desires the Spirit which He has made to dwell in us?" (James 4:4-5, NASB).

I cannot worship God while I am serving money. Otherwise, I am committing spiritual adultery. All idolatry bypasses a vital relationship with God. God is a jealous God, because spiritual adultery cripples our walk with Him. We must turn away from our idols.

Israel fell because of idolatry. Judah fell because of idolatry. Christians in America commit both kinds of idolatry. We are creating a new god, a god easy to understand, simple to approach, safe to manipulate. He is a new god, but we call him the Lord. We are also adopting other gods alongside the Lord, especially the gods of money and pleasure, and serving those gods while we also attempt to serve the Lord. Somehow we have fooled ourselves into thinking that God does not mind our adulterous affair with money.

American idolaters have created a false god of happiness and victory and renamed it the Lord. American idolaters have adopted the false gods of pleasure, wealth and success alongside the Lord. Yet in the midst of this, we still love to worship. We have fooled ourselves into thinking that the happier our religion is, the more we are experiencing God's presence; that the wealthier our churches

are, the greater the proof that God is with us. Samuel
Lamb, a Chinese Christian pastor who spent twenty
years in prison for the sake of the gospel, said this about
the situation in America: "Our churches in China are undergoing persecution; your churches in the West are undergoing delusion."

God, however, has not been deluded by our idolatry.
He speaks to our style of idolatry in Revelation 3:17-20:

> You say, "I am rich; I have acquired wealth and do not
> need a thing." But you do not realize that you are
> wretched, pitiful, poor, blind and naked. I counsel you
> to buy from me gold refined in the fire, so you can be-
> come rich; and white clothes to wear, so you can cover
> your shameful nakedness; and salve to put on your
> eyes, so you can see.
>
> Those whom I love I rebuke and discipline. So be
> earnest, and repent. Here I am! I stand at the door and
> knock. If anyone hears my voice and opens the door, I
> will come in and eat with him, and he with me.

*   *   *

Charles glanced at the clock again. It was 2:00 in the
morning, and he had been tossing and turning for hours. He
had been wondering all night, Could Sharlene be right? She
had attacked everything he held most dear in his walk with
God. Her last plea to him had pierced his heart. As they
were getting ready for bed, she reached out to him and held
him for a long time without saying a word. Then she looked
him directly in the eyes and said in a quiet voice, "Charles, if
you need music so badly that you can't find God without it,
what kind of God do you really serve?"

He grimaced as her words echoed through his mind. What kind of God do I serve? he wondered. Finally, he prayed a simple prayer. *Lord, show me from Your Word what kind of God I need to serve. Show me from Your Word.*

QUESTION:
How can I tell if I am committing idolatry?

PRINCIPLE 7:

B: I am committing idolatry when I seek to bypass my relationship with God in order to gain whatever I desire.

SIX

How Should I Worship
God in Song?

QUESTION:
How should I worship God in song?

PRINCIPLE 8:

A: Using the Psalms as my model, my songs should bring to God both my sorrows and my joys.

B: Using the Psalms as my model, I should focus my praise on who God is and what He does, rather than on how I feel about Him.

Troy's office, Saturday morning, March 3

Charles sat down across from Troy and sighed. "This has been a horrible week for me. On Tuesday, Sharlene and I had the worst argument we've had in twenty years. Well, it was hardly a real argument. But she really nailed me, and I can't stop thinking about what she said. That's why I'm here this morning."

He paused. Troy thought that Charles looked worn out, almost broken down. He waited for him to continue.

"Anyway," Charles said, "I have a question for you. What does the Bible teach about music and worship? I've been looking all over the place in the Bible, and I'm not finding anything much. It's really important to me."

Troy smiled. "Charles, if you had come to me three years ago, I would have given you a completely different answer. Then I started my own study of the Bible about music and worship. I found my answer in the Psalms. They are the clearest example of music in the Bible."

Slowly shaking his head, Charles replied, "I've been reading and reading the Psalms, Troy, but I just can't figure out how music fits in with them. How do I start?"

For Troy, the question brought back memories of nighttime studies in the Psalms that went on for months. He certainly understood Charles' frustration. Troy got up and walked over to his filing cabinet. He came to a folder and pulled out a paper labeled "Psalms Analysis" and handed it to Charles.

"I'd like to give you a challenge," Troy said. "This chart has every kind of statement you can find in the Psalms."

Charles looked over the chart. The first column was numbered from one to sixteen. The second column had sixteen different categories, such as "Appeal for God's help" or "Praise because of God's character." The third column explained the different categories. Charles looked up at Troy, perplexed.

Troy smiled at his confusion. "If you want to find out what the Bible teaches about music and worship, take about thirty of the Psalms and use this chart to categorize each verse of the psalm."

Charles nodded, but still looked doubtful. "What will that do?" he asked. "That still won't tell me what the Psalms teach about music and worship."

"I understand your question," Troy answered. "The real problem is that we seldom read or sing an entire psalm at once, so we don't really understand how David approached worship. Using this chart will help you to see the whole picture, what was really important when he wrote the psalm. I suspect that you'll find David used music a lot differently than you might think."

After a few minutes of conversation, Charles left. As he drove home, he wrestled with God. *Lord*, he prayed, *I came to Troy for answers, and all he gave me was this chart.*

Then a thought occurred to him. *I prayed for God to show me in His Word. Maybe this is exactly what I can use to find out what His Word says.*

He pulled into his driveway and parked his car. Bowing his head on the steering wheel, Charles took a step of faith. "Lord, help me to understand each psalm using this chart. Direct me into Your perfect will. Amen."

He opened the door and entered his house. He had his work cut out for him now.

David and Israel's Music

Charles came to Troy because Sharlene had challenged his entire concept of worship. Sharlene's question, "If you need music so badly that you can't find

God without it, what kind of God do you really serve?" shook the foundations of how he *served* God in worship. Charles believed that music helped him to feel God's presence, to touch God and know Him more personally. Now all of a sudden he realized that he didn't know how music related to worship.

When Christians in America engage in worship wars, they focus most on music styles. Other points of disagreement, such as raising hands, speaking in tongues or dancing in the Spirit, may divide churches, but none so often as music styles. We have already seen in chapter 4 that Moses did not give Israel any direction concerning the role of music in worship. Israel waited until David became king to learn God's blueprint for music and worship. His influence on Israel's worship music cannot be overstated.

David changed the way Israel worshiped. He was a skillful musician in his own right (1 Samuel 16:16-18). During his younger days, music was very much a part of Israel's celebration of great events (18:6-7). When he became king, David used music to celebrate the return of the ark of the covenant to Jerusalem. "David, wearing a linen ephod, danced before the LORD with all his might, while he and the entire house of Israel brought up the ark of the LORD with shouts and the sound of trumpets" (2 Samuel 6:14-15).

When David established the tabernacle in Jerusalem, he began creating the structures for music in worship. The Scriptures specifically credit David with appointing singers to sing before the tabernacle. "These are the men David put in charge of the music in the house of the LORD after the ark came to rest there. They ministered with music before the tabernacle, the Tent of Meeting, until Solomon built the temple of the LORD in Jerusalem. They performed their duties according to the regulations laid down for them" (1 Chronicles 6:31-32). He appointed them "to sing joyful songs" (15:16). They also blew musical instruments "before the ark of God" (15:24).

In addition, David set aside those who would prophesy using musical instruments. "David, together with the commanders of the army, set apart some of the sons of Asaph, Heman and Jeduthun for the ministry of prophesying, accompanied by harps, lyres and cymbals" (25:1). This meant "thanking and praising the LORD" (25:3). The fact that these singers were prophesying as they sang may suggest that God was giving them the words.

David standardized Israel's worship music. Centuries after he died, the priests still used his standards for musical instruments. "As the offering began, singing to the LORD began also, accompanied by trumpets and the instruments of David king of Israel" (2 Chronicles 29:27). David may have even designed the instruments himself.

> The priests took their positions, as did the Levites with the LORD's musical instruments, which King David had made for praising the LORD and which were used when he gave thanks. (7:6)

God Himself established the divinely appointed standards for the instruments through His prophets Nathan and Gad.

> He stationed the Levites in the temple of the LORD with cymbals, harps and lyres in the way prescribed by David and Gad the king's seer and Nathan the

prophet; this was commanded by the LORD through
his prophets. (29:25)

In addition to the words, singers and instruments, the
musical patterns were also divinely appointed. Many of
the musical instructions in the Psalms may refer to familiar melodies. Look at the titles of some of the Psalms before Psalm 88. Psalms 8, 81 and 84, for example, are "according to *gittith*" (*'al Gittith*), which may be a musical
tune name, a pattern or perhaps even a musical instru-
ment (scholars do not actually know how to translate the
word). Psalm 9 is *'al-muth labben,* perhaps another tune
name, which literally means "The Death of the Son."
There are several other possible tune names mentioned
in the Psalms, most of which David probably wrote. But
after Psalm 88, no more melodies are mentioned. Perhaps by then, the melodies were so standardized that
singers did not need instructions on specific melodies.

David's standards of music may even have influenced
the early Church. Musicologists have discovered isolated
groups of Jews in Yemen, Babylonia, Persia and Buchara
whose music is very ancient. Their Jewish song melodies,
which David may have written and standardized, are
similar to Christian Gregorian chants. This would make
sense, since we know that the Jews continued to follow
David's standards for music even after the exile. "When
the builders laid the foundation of the temple of the
LORD, the priests in their vestments and with trumpets,
and the Levites (the sons of Asaph) with cymbals, took
their places to praise the LORD, as prescribed by David
king of Israel" (Ezra 3:10).

The Scriptures never mention using musical instruments at the temple until the time of David. Further-

more, the Scriptures tell us that David established the
musical instruments for temple worship (1 Chronicles
23:5; 2 Chronicles 7:6; 29:27). David began these
things during his reign as king. After David's reign, sacrifices were accompanied by music, and singers used
designated psalms to accompany the individual feasts
and special celebrations.

The church today experiences David's influence on
worship through the Psalms. Seventy-seven of the 150
psalms begin with the inscription, "Of David," meaning that he likely wrote those particular psalms. It is
also possible that the writer composed the psalm to be
set to David's music or that the writer composed the
psalm according to the standards David set.

Troy suggested that Charles study the Psalms by cate-
gorizing each verse of many different psalms. The chart
he created would help Charles see the overall picture.
What did the psalmist really sing about? Troy's purpose
was for Charles to discover biblical principles of worship.
The Psalms offer a clear blueprint for approaching God in
worship. Troy's study method went beyond singing a few
inspirational snippets from any given psalm. It enabled
Charles to see the larger picture in David's worship.

I have based the following two principles upon a
careful analysis of many psalms in the Bible. Applying
each principle to our situation today would transform
our worship services.

Bring God Both Your Sorrows and Joy

The psalmists wrote as much or more about their grief
as they did about their times of exaltation. In fact, a com-
parison study shows that there are more verses about

pain in the Psalms than there are about exultation and praise. Contrast that with worship services today, which are shrouded in empty happiness. Hurting people who smile sweetly during the praise time are weeping in their hearts. Not so with the psalmists. They were unafraid to tell God all about their grief and despair. Remember, worship expresses our relationship with God, and the psalmists knew that their sorrows and fears were every bit as much a part of their relationship with God as their joy.

Sharlene experienced this principle in her struggle after the death of her son. She found her greatest joy in the midst of profound grief. That sounds like the experiences of the psalmists. Most often, when they praised or rejoiced, they were praising in the midst of their grief.

Psalm 42 is a perfect example. It begins with a beautiful picture of thirsting for God alone:

> As the deer pants for streams of water,
>   so my soul pants for you, O God.
> My soul thirsts for God, for the living God.
>   When can I go and meet with God? (42:1-2)

This passage forms the basis of a contemporary chorus, "As the Deer," by Martin J. Nystrom, which describes our thirst for a love relationship with God.

The chorus describes the passions of the heart, a divine romance with the precious One we love. It begins by comparing a deer's thirst for water to the singer's longing for God, his deepest desire. He aspires for God because the Lord alone can meet his profoundest needs. Nothing else in life, neither gold nor silver, suffices. Because "As the Deer" centers on the Christian's passion for God, it sounds very much like so many contemporary love songs. Ardent emotions fuel American

pop lyrics these days. The whole approach to worship
we see in so many worship choruses echoes the intense
feelings we hear in current love songs.

"As the Deer" is a beautiful song that is a favorite
among Christians and is sung often in churches across
America. There is nothing wrong with this love song. The
modern chorus, however, has little to do with the original
thought of Psalm 42. Let's look at the entire psalm in its
original setting.

The psalmist begins with the same three statements
we find in "As the Deer."

> As the deer pants for streams of water,
>   so my soul pants for you, O God.
> My soul thirsts for God, for the living God. (42:1-2)

Then he tells us why he thirsts for God. He has been
suffering great sorrow and pain.

> When can I go and meet with God?
> My tears have been my food
>   day and night,
> while men say to me all day long,
>   "Where is your God?"
> These things I remember
>   as I pour out my soul:
> how I used to go with the multitude,
>   leading the procession to the house of God,
> with shouts of joy and thanksgiving
>   among the festive throng. (42:2-4)

In the midst of the psalmist's sorrow, he looks within
and challenges himself. He must turn his heart to the
Lord.

> Why are you downcast, O my soul?
>   Why so disturbed within me?
> Put your hope in God,
>   for I will yet praise him,
>   my Savior and my God. (42:5-6)

At this point, the psalmist begins to appeal to God. He tells God about his despair.

> My soul is downcast within me;
>   therefore I will remember you
> from the land of the Jordan,
>   the heights of Hermon—from Mount Mizar.
> Deep calls to deep
>   in the roar of your waterfalls;
> all your waves and breakers
>   have swept over me. (42:6-7)

Then he again forces himself to remember that God is on his side.

> By day the LORD directs his love,
>   at night his song is with me—
>   a prayer to the God of my life. (42:8)

Therefore, because the psalmist suffers and because God cares, he begs God to answer him in his time of pain and sorrow.

> I say to God my Rock,
>   "Why have you forgotten me?
> Why must I go about mourning,
>   oppressed by the enemy?"
> My bones suffer mortal agony
>   as my foes taunt me,

saying to me all day long,
   'Where is your God?' " (42:9-10)

Finally, after describing his thirst for God and his deep suffering, and appealing to God for help, the psalmist forces his heart back to hope.

Why are you downcast, O my soul?
   Why so disturbed within me?
Put your hope in God,
   for I will yet praise him,
   my Savior and my God. (42:11)

Thirst, pain, sorrow, mourning. Things have not changed much from the days of David. When the psalmists sang, they brought these things to God and found hope in the midst of them. Imagine Sharlene in her sorrow over the death of Chris, her son. Which song would have comforted her more: "As the Deer" or Psalm 42? The answer is obvious. Psalm 42 describes the kinds of heartaches that every person faces in life. Psalm 42 teaches us how to turn to God in the midst of our sorrows and find comfort by hoping in Him. The contemporary chorus is pretty and stirs our emotions, but it often does not have enough depth. When pain fills our hearts, we need more than a love song to hold on to.

This first worship principle from the Psalms instructs us to understand each psalm the way it was originally intended to be understood—from beginning to end as a single unit. We often miss this in our times of worship. Some of our favorite hymns and choruses take the happy parts of a psalm and ignore the heartache. Yet the psalmist did not write his psalm simply to describe happy feelings. Psalmists found that joy most often comes in the midst of deep pain. Many joyful sections of psalms have very little meaning apart from the sorrow that produced them. Granted, we may not be able to read or sing all of the lengthy psalms, such as Psalm 119, in our services, but we can combine singing and reading to make sure that the real message of the psalm comes out.

QUESTION:
How should I worship God in song?

PRINCIPLE 8:

A: Using the Psalms as my model, my songs should bring to God both my sorrows and my joys.

Find Your Solutions in God Alone

Almost every psalm teaches us about God, His ways, His character and what He has done. A few psalms do not tell us much about these things; Psalms 148-150 are mostly psalms of exultation, for example. Almost every other psalm, however, reveals specific truths about God's ways and character. That's why the Psalms form a pro-found book of theology. The psalmists did not just feel emotions about God. They understood who He is. They thought about Him and contemplated Him and sang profound truths about the way He works. Much thought went into these beautiful and sometimes disturbing psalms. Songwriters today should work as diligently to produce songs that provoke such deep thought.

You may have experienced the kind of pain Sharlene underwent when her son was dying. When we endure that kind of sorrow, we reexamine our faith in God. What kind of God lets a young man waste away? What kind of love allows a godly Christian to suffer continually? Those questions drive us to look again at God's love, His wisdom and His faithfulness. When someone whom we love suffers, we try to understand eternal truths. We do not want pat answers. We want to understand who God really is and what His purposes are.

The psalmists continually asked those kinds of questions. Twelve times they cried out to God, "How long, O LORD?" They begged God to stop hiding His face from them. "How long, O LORD? Will you hide yourself forever? How long will your wrath burn like fire?" (Psalm 89:46).

They always answered their agonized pleas with the same approach. God is faithful. God is good. God is just. God's lovingkindness never ceases. God has heard in the past. Always their answer is "God is . . . God is . . . God is . . . ." God's character, faithfulness and justice underlie whatever comfort or hope the Psalms offer.

We must build our worship songs upon the same foundation. Our songs should be about God, His promises, His character, His actions in the past and His nature. There is little help in singing about how we feel about praising God. The psalmists rarely approached anything in such a shallow manner. They praised God in the midst of their fear, because He is a faithful Father, a wise Shepherd and a loving King, or because He had proven Himself again and again in the past. Many psalmists referred to God's promises to Abraham or

Moses. Regardless of the words they chose, the worship of the psalmists was not about how they felt about God but about the kind of God He is.

If you were suffering and a friend tried to comfort you by telling you to feel good about worshiping God, would that help you? On the other hand, if your friend reminded you of God's deep love for you, that would give you true comfort. Why? Because that's precisely what you need to understand, that God loves you. That is why God gave us the Psalms. Real people underwent real heartbreak in order to learn what God is really like. When the psalmists describe God's faithfulness, you listen to them because they learned these truths in the midst of their great pain.

Let us learn from the Psalms how to sing to God. Let us learn to grapple with the pain of life by focusing our thoughts on who God really is.

Focus Your Praise on God Himself

The Psalms can teach us much about praising and thanking God. For example, they mention giving thanks to God more than fifty times. And well more than 100 verses describe praising Him. Obviously, praise and thanksgiving need to drive our relationship with the Lord.

We can learn a remarkable lesson from the way the psalmists praised and thanked God. They thanked Him by describing what He is like and what He has done. Let's use Psalm 18:48-50 as one example of this.

First, David described what God did for him. "[He] saves me from my enemies. [He] exalted me above my foes; from violent men [He] rescued me" (18:48).

Next, David pledged that he would publicly thank and praise God. "Therefore I will praise you among the nations, O LORD; I will sing praises to your name" (18:49).

Then, David mentioned which things about God and His ways he would talk about when he thanked and praised Him publicly. "He gives his king great victories; he shows unfailing kindness to his anointed, to David and his descendants forever" (18:50).

Take almost any psalm that discusses praise or thanksgiving and you will find the same general statements: (1) This is what God is or does for us; (2) I will praise or thank Him publicly about these things.

The Psalms overflow with all kinds of mixed emotions. When they overflow with exultation or praise or thanksgiving, they talk about what God is like and what He does. In direct contrast, many hymns and choruses focus on *our* feelings about *our* praising God. The psalmists do that on rare occasions. Far more often, however, their praise or thanks is used to describe or exalt God.

Of course, part of the reason for this difference is cultural. American culture sees love as an emotional experience that comes and goes. In romance, I do not love you because of what you are but because of how you make me feel. Because sex is the ultimate *feeling* experience, it becomes the central expression of romantic love. When the feelings die, the relationship dies too.

Americans have transferred their (mis)understanding of love into their worship. Look at many of the worship songs being sung today. They focus on how we feel about worshiping God. Even when they simply say, "I praise You" or "I love You" or "I worship You" or "I thank You," they do not tell us anything about God Himself. They often mention the fact that He is glorious, awesome and powerful. They often tell us that He is worthy, but they do not tell us what about Him is worthy. In fact, change the names in many hymns and choruses, and the songs would sound like a contemporary love song. The shallowness of American romance has taken over our "romance" with God.

The psalmists, on the other hand, praised God for specific characteristics. God is righteous, just, kind, loving, wise, powerful, good, avenging, protecting and compassionate. They also praised Him for what God had done. In so doing, they moved the focus away from *how they felt* to *who God is* and *what He has done*. This is what we should do when we are in the midst of a trial. Continually reminding ourselves of what God is like enables us to take steps of faith in our relationship with Him. "You are like this," we say to Him. "Therefore, I can trust You today."

Using a chart similar to the one Troy gave Charles to study the Psalms teaches us to approach God the way David approached Him. A whole new way of praising God could open up to us. We would find that our favorite songs and hymns may have little in common with praise in the Bible. That discovery could lead us to wonder how well we are really praising God in our worship on Sunday mornings.

Emotions are not bad in and of themselves, but they do not last. That's why truth must lead our emotions, rather than our emotions teaching us truth. Loving God with all of our hearts means that we will never allow our emotions to dictate our relationship with Him. We learn to love His faithfulness and His kindness and His goodness. The Psalms teach us that when our emotions contradict what we have learned, we must force our emotions back to reality. Many times the psalmists confessed that they were afraid or discouraged or overwhelmed, but they always made themselves remember what God is like and what He had done. Truth, not emotion, directed their steps.

Q u e s t i o n :
How should I worship God in song?

P R I N C I P L E 8 :

B: Using the Psalms as my model, I should focus my praise on who God is and what He does, rather than on how I feel about Him.

---

*   *   *

That evening, when Charles sat down next to his wife on the couch, he had a strange look on his face. Sharlene looked at him so intently that he said to her, "What? What have I done?"

She kept looking at him. "What's going on, sweetheart? What in the world have you been doing all day?"

Charles picked up the notebook he had laid on the coffee table and opened it. "I've been studying the Psalms and I can't believe it."

His wife took the notebook and looked through it. She had a hard time making out what she was seeing. Handing it back, she asked, "What are you talking about?"

Her husband put on his reading glasses and began to read his handwritten chart. "Did you realize that the psalmists asked God to judge the wicked more than they praised Him? Did you know that the psalmists spent much more time talking about their suffering than talking about giving thanks to God?"

Sharlene tried to understand Charles' point, but could not quite grasp where he was heading. "Why are you telling me all of this?"

He put down the chart and took hold of his wife's hands. "Sharlene, the Psalms are not bright and cheerful. They question God, they accuse the wicked, they complain about their sufferings *and* they praise."

Still confused, Sharlene prodded her husband to continue. "And . . . the point of all this is . . . ?"

Charles smiled. "The point of all this is that you were right. When David worshiped God, he didn't spend much time on the happy songs. He spent most of his time bringing God his struggles with life. David's worship was like yours, learning about joy in the midst of pain."

"So what does that mean as far as our church goes?" Sharlene asked.

"It means," her husband replied, "that it's time to rethink my whole understanding of worshiping God. I have a lot of Bible reading to do in the next few days—a whole lot of reading."

SEVEN

What Did the Prophets Teach about Worship?

QUESTION:
What did the prophets teach about worship?

PRINCIPLE 9:

A: The prophets exposed Israel's idolatry and revealed why the people turned away from the Lord.

B: The prophets taught that God did not criticize Israel's methods of worship. He instead criticized the fact that the people's worship was not in truth, because they did not truly love God nor did they demonstrate love for their neighbors.

C: The prophets taught that God removed His presence from the temple right before Babylon destroyed it. God's presence would not return until the Messiah came.

D: The prophets taught that when the Messiah came, both Jew and Gentile would bring acceptable sacrifices to God in restored worship.

After church, Sunday, March 4

Troy and Isabelle drove home from church.

"I was so excited to see Fred and Janice in church this morning," Isabelle said. "Can you believe it? It's been a month since they've come!"

"I don't know, Isabelle. What good does it do for Fred to come to church if he refuses to face up to his own sin?"

Isabelle looked at her husband in surprise. "You mean you've never done that?"

"Well . . . come on, Isabelle! This is different."

She sat silently the rest of the trip home, deep in thought.

As they pulled into the driveway, Troy finally blurted out. "All right, what are you thinking? I know something is going on inside of your brain." He stopped the car and turned off the ignition.

"Honey," Isabelle said carefully, "you have some pretty strong feelings against Fred, don't you?"

Troy moaned. "Do you really think that?"

She continued. "I have a feeling, sweetheart, that you would rather have Fred stay away."

Troy's thoughts were jumbled. How could he sort out the reasons he felt this way about Fred? Troy didn't really want to deal with it, but he knew that he was afraid of Fred. After all, he had run the last worship minister out of town. What would he do to Troy?

He looked back at Isabelle. "OK, doctor, what do you prescribe?"

"Why not call Fred up and ask him to help you fix the lawnmower?"

His mind said no. His emotions said no. He kept silent.

Isabelle's voice took on a sense of urgency. "Troy, you are the worship leader of First Community Church. You've taught

me everything I know about God's requirements for true worship." She laid her hand on his arm. "You don't want anything
to keep God from working through your ministry. God is more
interested in your heart than your ministry, Troy."

Troy got out of the car, opened his wife's door and escorted
her inside the house. Then he flipped open the church direc-
tory lying on the desk. He dialed the number and held his
breath. Isabelle prayed.

"Hi, Fred, this is Troy Smith. I was wondering if you could
help me out with my lawnmower."

*   *   *

If Troy wanted to lead his congregation in worship, his
own heart had to be genuine. Worship is not sincere unless the worshiper's actions and motives are pure. In both
the Old and New Testaments, God measured the purity
of worship by how worshipers treated one another. This
is the foundation Moses laid for true worship in the Law.
When the prophets judged Israel's worship, they based
their evaluations upon the foundation revealed in the
Law.

To prepare for our studies of worship in the New Testament, we will briefly survey four significant worship
themes found in the prophetical books of the Old Testament. Each theme sets the stage for the coming of Jesus
Christ.

Theme 1: Prophecies against Idolatry

Most often, the prophets spoke out against Israel's
present-day worship, especially its idolatry. "You also
took the fine jewelry I gave you, the jewelry made of my
gold and silver, and you made for yourself male idols and

engaged in prostitution with them" (Ezekiel 16:17). Ezekiel's condemnation echoes throughout the prophets.

Christians struggling with worship wars could solve many of their problems by reading what the prophets wrote against idolatry. Jeremiah's diagnosis of Judah's idolatry, for example, exposes all of us.

> "Has a nation ever changed its gods?
>   (Yet they are not gods at all.)
> But my people have exchanged their Glory
>   for worthless idols.
> Be appalled at this, O heavens,
>   and shudder with great horror,"
>   declares the LORD.
> "My people have committed two sins:
> They have forsaken me,
>   the spring of living water,
> and have dug their own cisterns,
>   broken cisterns that cannot hold water."
>
> (Jeremiah 2:11-13)

In their arid environment, the Hebrews customarily built cisterns to conserve water for the dry months of the year. Jeremiah said that, spiritually, Judah had replaced God as its source of living water with the cisterns of idolatry. The idols, however, would not save the people, because they could not hold water. Thus, Judah was dying of thirst because the people had forsaken God, the "spring of living water."

We may not worship idols made of wood or stone, but how often we exchange God's glory for the empty cisterns of money, power, programs, status and secular learning! Sometimes we even exchange the living waters of a relationship with God for music and worship itself.

QUESTION:
What did the prophets teach about worship?

PRINCIPLE 9:

A: The prophets exposed Israel's idolatry and revealed why the people turned away from the Lord.

Theme 2: False Worship and True Worship

The prophets also attacked worship that came from false hearts. Their message is as relevant today as it was then: If we do not obey God, He will not accept our worship. Jeremiah wrote, "Your burnt offerings are not acceptable; your sacrifices do not please me" (Jeremiah 6:20). Amos said, "Even though you bring me burnt offerings and grain offerings, I will not accept them. Though you bring choice fellowship offerings, I will have no regard for them" (Amos 5:22). Hosea declared, "They offer sacrifices given to me and they eat the meat, but the LORD is not pleased with them" (Hosea 8:13). Micah wondered, "With what shall I come before the LORD and bow down before the exalted God? Shall I come before him with burnt offerings, with calves a year old? Will the LORD be pleased with thousands of rams, with ten thousand rivers of oil?" (Micah 6:6-7). Prophet after prophet condemned Israel and Judah for carrying on the rituals of worship without the heart of worship.

Isaiah 1:11-16 is a typical critique of God's distaste for empty worship.

> "The multitude of your sacrifices—
>   what are they to me?" says the LORD.
> "I have more than enough of burnt offerings,
>   of rams and the fat of fattened animals;
> I have no pleasure
>   in the blood of bulls and lambs and goats.
> When you come to appear before me,
>   who has asked this of you,
>   this trampling of my courts?
> Stop bringing meaningless offerings!
>   Your incense is detestable to me.
> New Moons, Sabbaths and convocations—
>   I cannot bear your evil assemblies.
> Your New Moon festivals and your appointed feasts
>   my soul hates.
> They have become a burden to me;
>   I am weary of bearing them.
> When you spread out your hands in prayer,
>   I will hide my eyes from you;
> even if you offer many prayers,
>   I will not listen.
> Your hands are full of blood;
>   wash and make yourselves clean."

The prophets judged the Israelites' worship by examining how they treated their neighbors. They almost never spoke out against Israel's failures to perform the rituals correctly. Instead, they spoke against hypocrisy.

If worshipers were unjust toward their brothers, the prophets denounced their worship as worthless.

> I hate, I despise your religious feasts;
> > I cannot stand your assemblies.
> Even though you bring me burnt offerings
> > and grain offerings,
> > I will not accept them.
> Though you bring choice fellowship offerings,
> > I will have no regard for them.
> Away with the noise of your songs!
> > I will not listen to the music of your harps.
> But let justice roll on like a river,
> > righteousness like a never-failing stream!
>
> > (Amos 5:21-24)

The prophets never separated worship from everyday life. The Hebrew worshiped God in part by the way he treated his brother. If he had clean hands—if he had practiced justice and mercy—then his worship was acceptable to the Lord. "Who may ascend the hill of the LORD? Who may stand in his holy place? He who has clean hands and a pure heart, who does not lift up his soul to an idol or swear by what is false" (Psalm 24:3-4). God never commanded a religion of rituals. He expected His worshipers to come to Him in truth. Just as He rejected Cain's false worship, so too He rejected any worship brought by false hearts.

What could be more ironic than First Community Church's worship war? The people fought among themselves to establish the kind of worship experience that they enjoyed the most. Yet God clearly reveals in His Word that worship is acceptable only when the hearts of the worshipers are cleansed. Fred's manipulation of the board defiled the worship of First Community Church. Perhaps even Charles' bitterness tarnished their songs of praise. The war itself made true worship impossible.

Q U E S T I O N :
What did the prophets teach about worship?

P R I N C I P L E 9 :

B: The prophets taught that God did not criticize Israel's methods of worship. He instead criticized the fact that the people's worship was not in truth, because they did not truly love God nor did they demonstrate love for their neighbors.

Theme 3: The Temple

Not only did the prophets deal with these moral problems in Israel's worship, but they also turned their eyes to the future. God revealed to many of the prophets that sometime in the future He would dramatically change Israel's experience. The Messiah would bring justice, judgment, restoration and a new and glorious kingdom (Jeremiah 33:14-18; Isaiah 11; and many other passages). We know this kingdom as the millennium (Revelation 20:1-10), a time when the Messiah will reign upon the earth with absolute power and universal glory (Isaiah 9:7). The land will be renewed and Israel will know God in a profoundly personal way (Jeremiah 31:31-40). Obviously, many of these future events will affect Israel's experience of worship, but one of the most significant ways will be in the future temple.

We need to understand what the prophets taught about the future temple for two reasons. First, the temple served as the central point of Israel's worship in the Old Testament. Since the temple is so important, we need to understand what the prophets proclaimed about the temple in the future. Second, many of the prophets' teachings about the new temple are fulfilled in the New Testament. Therefore, by understanding what the prophets taught about the temple, we will be able to understand how we should relate to the temple in our own worship today.

The earthly temple as a copy. The prophets saw the earthly temple as a copy of the heavenly one. "But the LORD is in his holy temple; let all the earth be silent before him" (Habakkuk 2:20). The heavenly temple is God's throne room. "In the year that King Uzziah died, I saw the Lord seated on a throne, high and exalted, and the train of his robe filled the temple" (Isaiah 6:1). We find this in the Psalms as well. "The LORD is in his holy temple; the LORD is on his heavenly throne" (Psalm 11:4).

The earthly Jerusalem temple, however, was also God's throne room. "A glorious throne, exalted from the beginning, is the place of our sanctuary" (Jeremiah 17:12). God ruled from His temple in heaven. He also ruled from His temple on earth.

The temple in the future. Fitting right into that theme, the prophets often described the temple's future millennial glory. In Malachi, the heavenly temple and the earthly temple almost seem to merge. " 'See, I will send my messenger, who will prepare the way before me. Then suddenly the

Lord you are seeking will come to his temple; the messenger of the covenant, whom you desire, will come,' says the LORD Almighty" (Malachi 3:1). Zechariah explained how that would be possible: The Messiah will sit as both priest and king on his throne in the temple.

> Tell him this is what the LORD Almighty says: "Here is the man whose name is the Branch, and he will branch out from his place and build the temple of the LORD. It is he who will build the temple of the LORD, and he will be clothed with majesty and will sit and rule on his throne. And he will be a priest on his throne. And there will be harmony between the two." (Zechariah 6:12-13)

Ezekiel 40-47 describes a temple beyond our present imagination. We cannot know if his treatment is symbolic or real, although at least part of the prophet's temple vision is symbolic (Ezekiel 47:1-12). Regardless, the prophets believed that the temple would be an important part of Israel's future.

The departure of God's glory from the temple. Ezekiel's vision of God's glory departing from the temple is the most chilling and important temple vision in the prophets. During the days immediately before Babylon destroyed the temple, Ezekiel saw God's glory move from the most holy place to the threshold of the temple (9:3). Judgment of Jerusalem began in terrifying detail. God's glory filled the temple the way it had filled it originally when Solomon dedicated it. Then the worst nightmare any pious Jew could dream unfolded.

> Then the glory of the LORD departed from over the threshold of the temple and stopped above the cherubim. While I watched, the cherubim spread their

> wings and rose from the ground, and as they went, the
> wheels went with them. They stopped at the entrance
> to the east gate of the LORD's house, and the glory of
> the God of Israel was above them. (10:18-19)

Soon God's presence had completely left the temple.

> Then the cherubim, with the wheels beside them,
> spread their wings, and the glory of the God of Israel
> was above them. The glory of the LORD went up
> from within the city and stopped above the moun-
> tain east of it. (11:22-23)

Putting this vision into its proper perspective prepares
us for worship in the future. God's glory departed from
the temple, the meeting place between God and man. Yet
Israel was a nation of priests to the entire world and the
temple was its place of worship. Once God's glory departed, the temple could not be a true meeting place between God and humankind. Until God's glory returned,
the temple would be an empty house.

QUESTION:
What did the prophets teach about worship?

PRINCIPLE 9:

C: The prophets taught that God removed His
presence from the temple right before Babylon
destroyed it. God's presence would not return
until the Messiah came.

Theme 4: Worship in the Future

Finally, the prophets laid the groundwork for the day when worship would be entirely new. They made astonishing promises that almost seem to come right out of the New Testament.

The coming of the Holy Spirit. First, they foretold the coming of God's Holy Spirit to His people. "I will give you a new heart and put a new spirit in you; I will remove from you your heart of stone and give you a heart of flesh. And I will put my Spirit in you and move you to follow my decrees and be careful to keep my laws" (Ezekiel 36:26-27). The Spirit would come to God's people in a way that was completely different from what had happened so far. "I will pour out my Spirit on your offspring, and my blessing on your descendants. They will spring up like grass in a meadow, like poplar trees by flowing streams" (Isaiah 44:3-4). What would it mean for worship when the Spirit came upon God's chosen people? Peter announced that promise of the Holy Spirit was fulfilled at Pentecost (Acts 2:16-18, quoting Joel 2:28-29).

Gentiles bringing offerings to the temple. Second, the prophets revealed that in God's millennial kingdom the Gentiles would offer sacrifices in the Jerusalem temple. This idea goes beyond anything a Jew would have imagined! "So the LORD will make himself known to the Egyptians, and in that day they will acknowledge the LORD. They will worship with sacrifices and grain offerings; they will make vows to the LORD and keep them" (Isaiah 19:21). God has already begun this prophecy's fulfillment through the worldwide proclamation of the gospel. For almost 2,000 years, at least some Egyptians have brought spiritual sacrifices to God as a result of the gospel of Jesus Christ. When God establishes the millennium, apparently those sacrifices will be offered in a literal temple in Jerusalem.

The future Messiah. These future promises were somehow tied together in the ministry of the Messiah. The Holy Spirit would anoint the Messiah's ministry. "The Spirit of the Sovereign LORD is on me, because the LORD has anointed me to preach good news to the poor" (Isaiah 61:1). The Messiah was to build the new temple. "It is he who will build the temple of the LORD, and he will be clothed with majesty and will . . . rule on his throne" (Zechariah 6:13). And the Gentiles would come to the Messiah in Jerusalem to be taught of God. "Many peoples will come and say, 'Come, let us go up to the mountain of the LORD, to the house of the God of Jacob. He will teach us his ways, so that we may walk in his paths' " (Isaiah 2:3).

Summing up the Prophets

When you read the prophets, look for the past, the present and the future. They founded their writings upon the past and especially on Moses' writings. Like Moses, the prophets judged worship by the worshiper's heart. They especially rejected worshipers who perverted justice and showed no compassion on the needy.

The prophets also looked to a future time when worship would include the Gentiles and would perfectly please God. God's glory departed from the first temple when He judged Israel. His glory would not return until the Messiah came. The future temple will be both God's and the Messiah's throne room on earth, just as the Old Testament temple was a copy of God's heavenly throne room.

From Abel to Malachi we consistently see the same themes. God wanted worshipers who worship Him in truth. God did not want rituals, but worshipers. The prophets never rejected the rituals taught by Moses. Some rituals were important because they already had meaning in that culture; for example, the *minhah* offerings, or bowing before God. Other rituals were important because they were pictures of God's heavenly throne room or of Jesus Christ on the cross. Still other rituals were important because they helped teach the Israelites, reminding them of God's gracious works in the past. Yet without the relationship, there was no point to the rituals.

If we learn anything from the Old Testament's theology of worship, it must be this: God is looking for those who worship Him in truth, without lies, without rebellion. True worship obeys God in all things. True worship loves one's brother and neighbor. True worship defends the widow and the orphan. True worship loves the stranger. With this remarkable foundation, we are ready to move to the New Testament's theology of worship.

Q U E S T I O N :
What did the prophets teach about worship?

P R I N C I P L E   9 :

D: The prophets taught that when the Messiah came, both Jew and Gentile would bring acceptable sacrifices to God in restored worship.

---

*   *   *

Monday evening, March 5

Troy came into the kitchen and sat down at the counter. Isabelle put down her book and looked at her husband. He seemed different, almost as if a burden had been taken off his shoulders.

Isabelle put her arm around her husband. "Well? How did your time over at Fred's house go?"

Troy looked down a while and then said vacantly, "Fine . . . "

She looked quizzically at her husband. "What are you thinking, Troy?"

He shrugged. "Fred's an OK guy."

Isabelle nodded. "And . . ."

"Fred's just an OK guy, Isabelle," he repeated. "What more do you want me to say?"

"Well," she asked, "what did you talk about?"

Troy shrugged his shoulders again. "The gas leak on the lawn mower."

Isabelle looked surprised. "That's it?"

He nodded his head. "Yeah, that's it. That's enough, isn't it? After all, I thought that Fred was some kind of Nazi or something. He isn't. He's . . ."

Isabelle finished for him. "An OK guy?"

"Yeah."

Troy stared for a long while at the table, deep in thought. Isabelle waited, wondering what her husband was thinking.

"You know, Isabelle, I've been a real hypocrite. All this time I thought that First Community Church was so sinful because they hated each other. And the whole time I was hating Fred just as much. And I didn't even know him!"

Shaking his head, he continued, "I hope we don't have anything planned for Thursday evening, because Fred and Janice are coming over here for dinner."

Isabelle smiled. "No, we don't have anything going."

"Good," her husband replied. "I'd like you to get to know Fred. He's an OK guy."

EIGHT

Now That Jesus Has Come, How Do I Come to God to Worship Him?

QUESTION:
Now that Jesus has come,
how do I come to God to worship Him?

PRINCIPLE 10:

A: Jesus taught that He is the New Temple, so I must come to Jesus Himself in order to worship God.

B: Jesus taught that He is the replacement and fulfillment of all of Israel's feasts and rituals of worship. I must come to Jesus to experience the true meaning of Israel's religion.

Fred and Janice's house, Monday evening, March 5

Fred came in and sat down at the kitchen table. Janice looked over at him, surprised to see him smiling.

"What's going on?" she asked curiously.

"Well," he said, "we're going over to the Smiths' on Thursday evening for dinner."

Janice was shocked. "You're kidding! I was surprised enough that you helped Troy with his lawn mower."

Fred nodded. "Yeah, I know. But at least Troy isn't some kind of flaming charismatic. Not like Pastor Rick was, anyway."

"Rick was not exactly a charismatic. He was just really into worship."

Fred frowned. "I always felt as if Rick was pushing us or something. Every week we had to have this worship experience or else we didn't really know God. I hated it."

"Maybe it was his music," his wife replied. "If he was leading us in old-time hymns, you'd wouldn't have had a problem with him."

Fred sighed. "I don't know, Janice. It was more than the music. It was the emotional thing. It was as if he wanted us to *feel* God's presence. I know that I love the Lord. I just don't have a lot of emotions. I never have. Rick made me feel like a phony Christian or something. I hated it."

Janice understood. She had never liked being forced to stand for twenty straight minutes to sing. She never liked being chided because she didn't clap her hands or raise them during the choruses. She felt so uncomfortable during the worship time.

Both of them began dreading attending church and would jump at any excuse to skip. Fred even occasionally volunteered in the nursery just to avoid being in the services.

He sat silent at the table for a long time, thinking. Janice came over and began rubbing his shoulders. "What are you thinking, honey?"

"What is Pastor Rick doing these days, anyway?"

"I think that he's working for his father in the paper mill," Janice said. "I heard that they were pretty broken up by the whole thing, Fred."

Fred sighed. "Yeah, that's what I heard too." He sat for a moment in silence. "That's why I went over to Troy's to-night. I feel kind of bad about what happened to Rick. I just don't know what to do about it."

* * *

Fred and Janice's struggle about worship highlights a very important question. How do we "experience God" in New Testament worship?

We can't give a quick and easy answer to this, because the issues are very complex. When Jesus came to Israel, the Jews thought that they had a clear understanding of what it meant to experience God. They brought their sac-rifices to the temple. The father led the family in the Passover Seder. The children recited their Torah lessons. The community walked to the synagogue on the Sab-bath. They knew what God required, and they followed those requirements to the best of their ability.

Jesus, however, threw their carefully regulated religion into seeming anarchy. On the one hand, He lived like a Jew and worshiped like a Jew. His claims about Himself, however, entirely challenged the Jewish religion.

In many ways, Rick's semi-charismatic worship style did the same thing to Fred and Janice. They had a set way of coming to church, singing hymns and praising God. When Rick came, he challenged their relationship with

God by throwing those set ways aside. He brought a completely different approach. Pastor Rick wanted them to "experience God" through worship. Fred and Janice did not come to church for that purpose. They resisted Rick because his approach to worship questioned their relationship with God. They did not like that.

The leaders of Judaism did not like Jesus either. They did not particularly oppose His religion, although His lack of respect for the Sabbath sometimes deeply offended them. What they opposed about Jesus was His claim of how He Himself related to their religion. By studying Jesus' relationship to religion in general, we will be able to understand how to help people such as Fred and Janice in their struggle with Rick and his worship style.

Jesus Is the New Temple

Every devout Jew dreamed of bringing sacrifices to the temple in Jerusalem, especially at Passover. The temple stood at the center of Jewish devotion. We have seen that God required sacrifices to enable sinners to stand before Him. Those sacrifices could be offered only in the temple. That alone put the temple at the pinnacle in Jewish devotion.

When Jesus came to the temple in John 2:13-22, he made a whip of cords and drove out the money changers and the animals for sacrifice.

He struck at the core of Judaism by attacking the Jews' temple. When they questioned His authority, Jesus said to them, "Destroy this temple, and I will raise it again in three days" (2:19). Of course, no Jew would ever destroy the temple. It was the core of Judaism, the holiest place in the world. Jesus, however, was not speaking of the building. "But the temple he had spoken of was his body" (2:21). The true temple was no longer a building but Jesus' body. He had replaced the old with something entirely new.

Why did Jesus challenge the Jews' religion by removing from them the most important of all realities in their faith, the holy temple of God? Recall that the temple was holy because it was the place of sacrifice. Yet temple sacrifices were holy only because they prepared the way for the true Sacrifice, the Lamb of God, Jesus Christ. No longer could Jews seek cleansing from sin through a beautiful building in Jerusalem. Now they had to turn to the one true Sacrifice, the final 'ola. The temple sacrifices could no longer cleanse from sin once Jesus appeared. Destroy this temple, My body, He challenged, and I will raise it up to be the true and final temple.

With that statement, Jesus completely transformed Jewish religion from a religious experience to a body, the body of Jesus. From that point on, no Jew—or Gentile either—could find God in the marble wonder of Jerusalem. The sacrifices, the incense, the offerings, the prayers, the chants and the songs no longer opened the way to heaven. Now the Jews had to come to a New Temple, the body of Jesus Christ.

This body, the body of Jesus, was Paul's religion as well.

> Therefore do not let anyone judge you by what you eat or drink, or with regard to a religious festival, a New Moon celebration or a Sabbath day. These are a shadow of the things that were to come; the reality, however, is found in Christ. Do not let anyone who

delights in false humility and the worship of angels
disqualify you for the prize. Such a person goes into
great detail about what he has seen, and his unspiri-
tual mind puffs him up with idle notions. He has lost
connection with the Head, from whom the whole
body, supported and held together by its ligaments
and sinews, grows as God causes it to grow.
(Colossians 2:16-19)

Paul talked in this passage about food, drink, festivals,
New Moons and Sabbaths. These practices are the very
heart of religion. Religious people build their faith
around what they eat and drink, how they celebrate and
the kinds of practices they observe. Their services,
prayers, songs, feasts and worship form the sum of their
religion. Yet Paul called those things a shadow of what is
to come. Once the substance of faith comes, all of the
shadows dissipate.

Fred and Janice struggled because Rick's style called
their religion into question. Perhaps they would have
struggled with Jesus when He came almost 2,000 years
ago. Perhaps Jesus would have offended them when He
took away their religion of hymns and sermons. Now
that He has come to us, we meet God not in a worship
service, but in a person, the Person of Jesus Christ. Furthermore, we do not find God through our hymns and
songs but through His cross. As Paul said, "I resolved to
know nothing while I was with you except Jesus Christ
and him crucified" (1 Corinthians 2:2). The Christian
does not want to know the ways of religion, but the Person of Jesus Christ crucified. The Christian does not want
to know the ways of religion, but how to make Christ's
cross the driving force of life. This is why Jesus said that

day, "Destroy this temple, and I will raise it again in three days."

QUESTION:
Now that Jesus has come,
how do I come to God to worship Him?

PRINCIPLE 10:

A: Jesus taught that He is the New Temple, so I must come to Jesus Himself in order to worship God.

Jesus Replaces Every Feast

Pastor Rick's approach to worship offended Fred and Janice because it took away their familiar religious practices and replaced them with something new. Rick threw out the hymnbook and brought in passion-filled music and choruses. He wanted to replace their comfortable traditions with an experience of God.

Jesus did the same thing 2,000 years ago. We have seen that God ordained certain times as festivals to remember His gracious work in the past. God commanded that all of Israel gather in Jerusalem to celebrate Passover and the Feast of Unleavened Bread, for example. During that week they could look back on what He had done for them through Moses. They realized that they could always depend upon His promises if they were faithful to His covenant. These times of remembering served as important foundations of faith for each Jew.

Jesus, however, completely undercut their festivals and celebrations. He proclaimed Himself as the meaning of every feast, every required celebration. When the people gathered for the last day of the Feast of Tabernacles, for example, "Jesus stood and said in a loud voice, 'If anyone is thirsty, let him come to me and drink. Whoever believes in me, as the Scripture has said, streams of living water will flow from within him' " (John 7:37-38). On the last day of this feast, the priests would lead the people in a procession from the temple to the Pool of Siloam, drawing water to be poured out in remembrance of the wilderness wanderings. When Jesus cried out for them to drink from Him, He was saying to them that they should find the meaning of the feast in Him. He was the real Feast of Tabernacles and the Holy Spirit was the living water flowing out of every believer. "By this he meant the Spirit, whom those who believed in him were later to receive. Up to that time the Spirit had not been given, since Jesus had not yet been glorified" (7:39).

Jesus replaced even the Passover, perhaps the greatest feast of Israel. That last night, when Jesus sat with His disciples in the upper room, He took the elements of the Passover, the bread and the wine, and told His disciples that they were really His body. Just as the temple was really about His body, just as the Feast of Tabernacles was really about His body, so also the Passover was really about His body. Imagine telling a Jew that what he considered as his religion no longer had any meaning. Imagine telling a Jew that those practices most precious to him, which stirred his religious emotions most deeply, were for all intents and purposes finished. Imagine telling a Jew that a body, the body of

Jesus, had replaced his Passover, his Feast of Tabernacles and his Day of Atonement. Jesus replaced even the
daily sacrifices with His own body.

Jesus replaced Israel's experience of God with Himself.
Now in order to meet with God, the Jews had to go outside of the temple. They would not find God in the great
ceremonies of Tabernacles. They would not commune
with God at the Passover table. Instead, they had to
come to God through the Person of Jesus Christ. Not
through rituals. Not through festivals. Not through ob-
servances. Not through fasting. Not even through prayer,
singing, meditating or hungering. Only through Jesus.

Once we meet Jesus, we do not need religious experiences any longer. "Philip said, 'Lord, show us the Father
and that will be enough for us.' Jesus answered: 'Don't
you know me, Philip, even after I have been among you
such a long time? Anyone who has seen me has seen the
Father. How can you say, "Show us the Father"?' " (John
14:8-9). What had Philip expected Jesus to show them
that night? Was he looking for God to reveal His glory to
them the way He revealed it to Moses in Exodus 34?

Jesus rebuked him. The Man seated before Philip, who
was born of a virgin, who was about to suffer at the hands
of sinners, was the ultimate revelation of the Father.
"The Word became flesh and made his dwelling among
us. We have seen his glory, the glory of the One and
Only, who came from the Father, full of grace and truth"
(John 1:14). Moses had not truly seen God that day the
glory passed before him. "No one has ever seen God, but
God the One and Only, who is at the Father's side, has
made him known" (1:18). Philip, however, *had* seen God.
He had touched God. "That which was from the begin-

ning, which we have heard, which we have seen with our eyes, which we have looked at and our hands have touched—this we proclaim concerning the Word of life" (1 John 1:1). Philip had heard God speak, followed God and known Him.

This is why Fred and Janice were probably wrong in holding on to their religion of hymns. Since Jesus has come, religion no longer has any substance. We meet God in the Person of Jesus Christ. Later on we will discuss why Christians sing songs and meet together. For now, know that we no longer seek God through the experiences of religion. We now seek Him through Jesus Christ Himself, for Jesus has replaced all religion.

Pastor Rick also had made a profound mistake. He threw out Fred and Janice's religion, but substituted his own religion in its place. Rick wanted to experience God through a time of worship. He introduced love songs to Jesus accompanied by intense music. By creating an atmosphere of worship, he believed that First Community Church could experience God's presence. When people cooperated by raising their hands, joining in the spirit of the hour and seeking to "find" God, they underwent a profound religious experience. Rick believed that they were meeting with God.

When the Jews celebrated the Feast of Tabernacles, they probably also had something of a religious experience. Jesus, however, told them that their religious experience was no longer relevant. His body was now their Feast of Tabernacles. His body was now their holy temple. His body was now their Passover Seder. They could meet with God in the Person of Jesus and in Him alone. The fervor of their worship no longer brought them into God's presence. Rather, their faith in Jesus, the living Son of God, brought them into the throne room. To know Jesus was now to know God. To meet Jesus was now to meet God. We no longer need the trappings of religious experience to deepen our knowledge of God. We know Jesus through faith and through Him we are in the presence of the living God.

The arguments over worship most often miss this point. Christians today worship God in order to experience His presence, His touch. But you won't find this concept taught in the Bible. Worship leaders often invite Jesus' presence to be among us when we worship Him. Yet God already has poured out His Spirit into our beings. We are seated with Jesus in the heavenly places. This mystery, "which is Christ in you, the hope of glory" (Colossians 1:27), means that we have God's presence indwelling each one of us. The Scriptures promise no more of God's presence than that. Short of dying and going to heaven, how could there be more?

How, then, do we meet with Jesus? We meet Him through faith, not emotion. That faith trusts what God has said about Himself. That faith believes what He has said about us. More than anything, that faith embraces what He told us Himself: " 'But I, when I am lifted up from the earth, will draw all men to myself.' He said this to show the kind of death he was going to die" (John 12:32-33). Faith comes to Jesus through His cross.

Noah came to Jesus through the cross. He brought to God an 'ola sacrifice, which was a true picture of Jesus' cross. Abraham also came to Jesus through the cross. He brought his sinful son Isaac to Mount Moriah, to the place where Jesus Himself would die, and found a ram to take Isaac's place in death. That ram was a picture of Jesus' cross. Those Hebrews who brought their sacrifices to the temple, who knew their own sin and deeply desired to be cleansed, who humbly laid their hands upon the victim in repentance and then slew the animal, met Jesus through the cross. They believed, without knowing the name and time, that God had provided for them a Substitute to die in their place for their sin.

All of their religion—feasts, Sabbaths, songs and sacrifice—pointed to Jesus. To have Jesus is to have within our beings all that religion could only promise as a shadowy future. We need not sing to touch God, for He dwells within us. We need not fast to know God, for we sit beside Him in His heavenly throne room. We need no passion to find God's presence, for we meet Him by faith at the cross.

QUESTION:
Now that Jesus has come,
how do I come to God to worship Him?

PRINCIPLE 10:

B: Jesus taught that He is the replacement and fulfillment of all of Israel's feasts and rituals of worship. I must come to Jesus to experience the true meaning of Israel's religion.

---

*   *   *

Janice was worried. All evening Fred had sat in his chair, staring at the wall. She did not know that her husband was thinking about something Troy had said to him while they were working on the lawn mower.

"You know, Fred," Troy had said in a very uncomfortable voice, "I'm really sorry that I've been avoiding you. You scared me and I didn't want to get to know you. I was even glad when you stopped coming to church. I realize now how wrong that was."

At first the words were painful, because Fred felt that Troy had not given him a chance. As the evening wore on, however, Fred thought more and more about Pastor Rick and how glad he was that Rick had left the church. If it was wrong for Troy to be glad about Fred and Janice staying away from church, what about his feelings toward Pastor Rick? And if it was wrong to be glad that Rick was gone, what did that say about why he left? Just entertaining the thought opened up for Fred a frightening possibility: Had he sinned against Pastor Rick?

If he had sinned in engineering Rick's departure, then Rick should have stayed. Fred had been sure that Rick was wrong; he was sure that God did not want Rick in the church. But if Fred had sinned, maybe he was wrong about that too. Maybe God did want Rick to be their worship leader. Maybe Fred did not really know God. Maybe . . .

Up until that evening, Fred had always pushed those thoughts into the farthest corner of his mind. For some reason, they refused to stay hidden that night. Finally, Fred began to pray. *Lord, did I sin? Did I sin against You with Pastor Rick?* By even asking the question, he knew the answer. The hardest part came next. Fred needed to ask Jesus to cleanse him from these sins. He was going to have to face each one of them and admit to God that he had been wrong.

Fred sat there long after Janice went bed. He did not know whether Rick was right or not, and this profoundly disturbed him. What he did know is that he had been wrong, very wrong, in the way he had dealt with Rick. Tomorrow he would need to call the pastor and figure out how to heal this mess. Right now, however, he found the realization of his sin to be more painful than the entire episode with Rick had ever been. God seemed to be showing him sin after sin that he had committed against the pastor, the church, Rick and his wife, Jeri, and even Janice.

Fred realized that it didn't matter now whether he was right or wrong about Rick's approach to worship. His sin made whatever else he knew or did irrelevant. Until he completely dealt with that, nothing else mattered. Dealing with his sin, however, was going to be very painful.

NINE

How Do I Worship in Spirit and Truth?

QUESTION:
How do I worship in spirit and truth?

PRINCIPLE 11:

A: Only those who are born of the Spirit can worship God in spirit and truth.

B: I can sense the Spirit's working in my worship only through the results of what He does, for His presence and work among believers are mysterious.

C: I worship in truth when the Holy Spirit's fruit (love, joy, peace, patience, kindness, goodness, faithfulness, gentleness and self-control) accompanies my worship.

Pastor's study, Tuesday evening, March 6

Jeff opened his Bible to John 4:24 and began to read to Charles. "God is spirit, and his worshipers must worship in spirit and in truth."

Charles shook his head. "Pastor, I can't figure that passage out. I always thought that worshiping in spirit and truth meant the experience I undergo when worship time has been particularly powerful."

Jeff nodded. He had always felt the same way. Lately, however, he had begun to wonder if his understanding of the Spirit matched up with the Scriptures.

Troy was the one who had unsettled Jeff's understanding of the Holy Spirit. Two weeks ago, the two pastors had sat down to reevaluate where the church was headed. They had not yet brought music back into their worship services. They were watching the congregation dwindling, but wondered how much of that would have happened anyway. Several families had left, saying that the service was too boring. Troy was working hard at bringing interesting elements into the service, yet he could not create the kind of atmosphere that music brings into a worship time.

During their meeting, Jeff suggested that they abandon the plan that he had set up a few weeks before. *How much longer,* he wondered, *would our people stick it out?*

Troy understood Jeff's concerns, since he was struggling with the same fear. The worship minister, however, challenged Jeff with one thought before dropping their plan. "Change the plan, Jeff, if you believe the Spirit has worked in our congregation more through singing than without it."

Troy's question threw Jeff. It was obvious to anyone that the Spirit of God was working at First Community Church. He suspected that part of that spiritual growth came through the

worship time, because it was so focused now. Regardless, Jeff
knew that for the first time since he had been pastor, many
members were growing, dealing with sin, wrestling with the
sermons in an attempt to apply what Jeff was preaching, and
committing themselves to sacrificial ministry.

Even the fact that Charles was sitting across from Jeff this
evening meant that God was working. Before, Charles never
would have come to him for counsel. This was just one of a
whole series of evidences that the Spirit had been working
among them. The signs were not always dramatic, yet the fruit
was very real.

Troy's question two weeks before had prompted Jeff to
study the Word about the Spirit's work. Now, strangely,
Charles sat across from him asking him to explain the very
passage with which Jeff had wrestled the most. What did it
mean to worship in spirit and truth?

He looked up at Charles and smiled. "Well, Charles, I
would like to ask you a question. Do you believe the Spirit
has worked in our congregation more through singing or
without it?"

* * *

Pastor Jeff's struggle underlines how difficult it is to
understand worship in the light of Christ's coming. Before Jesus came, God commanded His people to worship Him in three ways. First, God commanded them
to serve Him through offerings and sacrifices. Second,
God commanded His people to remember. He established feasts, set aside the Sabbath and prescribed how
the people were to live and dress. Third, God commanded that they love Him and their neighbors. God
rejected their worship if they did not love their neighbors. Through these commandments, Jews understood

the nature of worship. They knew what they needed to bring to God and how they needed to bring it.

When Jesus came, He replaced the offerings and sacrifices (Hebrews 10:9-10). Furthermore, Jesus replaced Israel's feasts (1 Corinthians 5:7). Because of the changes Jesus brought, our understanding of worship has become much more complex. What kind of worship does God seek, now that Christ has come?

Jesus addressed that question when He spoke with the woman at the well. She was a Samaritan, and Samaritans believed that true worshipers must present their sacrifices on Mount Gerizim, not Jerusalem. "Our fathers worshiped on this mountain, but you Jews claim that the place where we must worship is in Jerusalem," she said to Jesus (John 4:20). In reply, Jesus told her that the Samaritans were wrong and that the Jews had the proper place for worship. "You Samaritans worship what you do not know; we worship what we do know, for salvation is from the Jews" (4:22).

Jesus completely shocked the woman when He said to her, "Believe me, woman, a time is coming when you will worship the Father neither on this mountain nor in Jerusalem" (4:21). God was changing His requirements for worship, so that Jerusalem would no longer be important. Once Jesus, the final Sacrifice, died on the cross, worship could be offered anywhere and at anytime. "Yet a time is coming and has now come when the true worshipers will worship the Father in spirit and truth, for they are the kind of worshipers the Father seeks" (4:23). Not only would the location, Jerusalem, be irrelevant, but the very heart of worship—sacrifices and offerings, Sabbaths and feasts, prayers and songs—also would change.

God Seeks Worshipers Who Are Born of the Spirit

What does it mean to worship in spirit and truth? Jesus told the woman that worshiping in spirit had something to do with the fact that God is spirit and humans are flesh. "God is spirit, and his worshipers must worship in spirit and in truth" (John 4:24). Human descendants of Adam and Eve are flesh by nature. "Flesh gives birth to flesh, but the Spirit gives birth to spirit" (3:6). Jesus was bringing humans into a new kind of existence, a second birth. No longer would we belong to Adam and Eve's world, the world of flesh. Now those who received Christ would belong to God's world, the world of the Spirit of God. Jesus said to Nicodemus, "I tell you the truth, no one can enter the kingdom of God unless he is born of water and the Spirit" (3:5).

The change Jesus brought to worship began with this transformation. Only those worshipers who are born of the Spirit can worship God in spirit and truth. Worshipers who belong to the flesh can only worship according to the flesh. For example, before Paul's conversion, everything he did in worship and service to God was according to the flesh.

> If anyone else thinks he has reasons to put confidence in the flesh, I have more: circumcised on the eighth day, of the people of Israel, of the tribe of Benjamin, a Hebrew of Hebrews; in regard to the law, a Pharisee; as for zeal, persecuting the church; as for legalistic righteousness, faultless. (Philippians 3:4-6)

He fulfilled all of the requirements of the Law. He brought all of the proper sacrifices and offerings. Yet all that he did was according to the flesh, because Paul was not yet born of the Spirit. God seeks worshipers who are born of the Spirit.

Surely no one at First Community Church would deny that true worshipers must be born of the Spirit. They would agree that those who are not born of the Spirit cannot know God. They might not realize, however, that many people in other religions have very profound religious experiences. Often those experiences feel the same as our own times of worship.

During my atheistic college years, I attended a Hindu Yoga service and watched the "worship." Toward the end of the very passionate mantra chanting, someone began to sing a "Christian" chorus, "Alleluia." Soon the entire room of 200 or so people joined in. Holding each other's hands, or lifting their hands in typical Yoga style, many swayed back and forth, while I watched in distrust. Not long after that, Jesus Christ transformed my life and I was born again. Ironically, I often sang that song during the years that followed without ever thinking about the first time I heard it. The feelings I felt as I sang it were the same feelings that all of those Hindu mantra chanters experienced when they sang it. I am certain that they were not encountering God's presence through singing that song because they were not born of the Spirit.

QUESTION:
How do I worship in spirit and truth?

PRINCIPLE 11:

A: Only those who are born of the Spirit can worship God in spirit and truth.

What the Spirit Does Is Often Mysterious

If Christians have similar worship experiences as those who are not born of the Spirit, how can we tell if we are worshiping in spirit and truth?

It is impossible to say that the Spirit is moving among a group of people simply because they are having a worship experience. The Spirit works in mysterious ways, often in ways that defy our senses.

In the Old Testament, worship worked through the senses. Worship engaged the sacrificer's senses—sight, touch, hearing and smell—in understanding sin and the cross. He would lay his hands upon the sacrifice, putting it to death and preparing it for the priest. The animal would cry out as the worshiper slaughtered it. He saw and felt the blood on his own hands. Worship was a very physical experience.

Holy days, such as feasts and Sabbaths, involved worshipers in physical activities to help them remember God's deliverance and His character. Even the music introduced by David involved them in worshiping God through a sensory experience.

Now, however, we are to worship in the Spirit. How does the Spirit work in our worship? Jesus told us that the Holy Spirit works the way wind in a desert land might work. "The wind blows wherever it pleases. You hear its sound, but you cannot tell where it comes from or where it is going. So it is with everyone born of the Spirit" (John 3:8). We may be able to see the effects of what He is doing among us, but we cannot see the Spirit Himself. Much of what He does among us begins and ends in secret and mystery.

Jesus used similar language to describe the way His words work. "The Spirit gives life; the flesh counts for nothing. The words I have spoken to you are spirit and they are life" (John 6:63). The Spirit of God anoints Jesus' words, so that they are spirit and life. Yet we cannot see the Spirit in God's words. We cannot see life in God's words. The life and the Spirit are like the wind. We can see the effect of what the Spirit and life are doing in our lives and in the lives of others through Jesus' words, but we cannot see the power.

Christians often try to turn the Holy Spirit into something they can see, feel, touch and even control. The Holy Spirit, however, is a Person, not a power, presence, force or feeling. He is the living God. We cannot "plug into the Spirit." He can come to us, but we cannot make it happen. He does whatever He pleases, for He is God.

Furthermore, we cannot pin down the Spirit's presence among us to any one feeling or any one experience. Remember, we can see the effects or the results of the work He does, but we do not see Him. He can show Himself in our times of worship by touching our emotions. Just as often, however, He can show Himself in our times of worship by convicting us of sin. Both are the Spirit's work. We dare not assume that when the Spirit touches our emotions that He is more present than when He convicts of sin. Both reveal that the Spirit is working. And the fact that He is at work in us opens a new way of worship.

The Holy Spirit's work brings us to an entirely new understanding of worship, as Jesus explained to the woman at the well. Until Christ came, worshipers carried lambs, doves, bulls and grain offerings to the temple, following a myriad of strict Levitical requirements. With Christ all of that changed. Now worshipers must bring their lives as offerings (Romans 12:1) to a new temple, the temple of the Holy Spirit (1 Peter 2:4-6; Ephesians 2:19-22). Now the Spirit Himself sanctifies those lives, making them pleasing and acceptable sacrifices (Romans 15:16; 1 Peter 1:2). Worshiping in spirit and truth removes the worshiper from the temple constructed by Law and from bringing sacrifices required by Law. Now we come to a temple of the Spirit and bring spiritual sacrifices. Wherever the Spirit is, there we find our place of worship (Philippians 3:3). We need no goats, no bulls, no incense, no earthly temple. We worship in the Spirit.

But how does the Spirit of God work to sanctify our offerings? When Troy took music away from the worship service, Charles felt as if God's presence had left. He assumed that God was not working in power because he did not *feel* anything. The entire battle over worship in First Community Church could have been avoided if everyone had agreed that they could not confine the Spirit's presence to any one experience. The Holy Spirit might have been working just as powerfully when there was no music or when the music did not stir everyone's emotions.

Does the Spirit ever work in other ways? We know that He often teaches us through our suffering (see 2 Corinthians 12, Hebrews 12 and James 1). We may ask God to heal us, but in order to instruct us He may choose not to heal. Does not His silence show us that He is working? The Old Testament teaches that it is good to wait for the Lord. "Be still before the LORD and wait patiently for him; do not fret when men succeed in their ways, when they carry out their wicked schemes" (Psalm 37:7). Does not the Spirit's work in making us wait also show us that He is present? We cannot see His power, His plans or His purposes—we see only the effects of what He does.

Until Pastor Rick pushed the church into a worship war, Jeff had always assumed that the emotional experience he encountered during singing was the presence of the Holy Spirit. His mistake is common. He did not realize that the Holy Spirit shows His presence among us in a multitude of ways. Now he was beginning to realize that God often works in ways we cannot feel emotionally or detect with our senses.

Therefore, we do not want to limit worshiping God in spirit and truth to any one effect. In a worship service, the Spirit of God is uniquely working with each individual believer, and we cannot see what He is doing. He may be giving one believer an experience of emotional exultation while bringing grief into the heart of another. All we can see are the results of what He does, but while He is doing it, His work remains a mystery.

More than anything, this must be Jeff's answer to Charles: The Spirit works as He wills. We must stop limiting the Holy Spirit to a feeling or an emotional experience. We must allow Him to do that, if that is the effect He wishes to produce.

QUESTION:
How do I worship in spirit and truth?

PRINCIPLE 11:

B: I can sense the Spirit's working in my worship only through the results of what He does, for His presence and work among believers are mysterious.

Worshiping God in Truth

Principle 11b describes what the Holy Spirit Himself does in sanctifying our offerings of worship. The next principle explains how we respond to what the Spirit of God is doing, for we must worship in spirit and *truth*. The Holy Spirit is the location of our worship. Our godly and sincere lives demonstrate the truth of our worship.

We have learned from our studies in the prophets what worshiping in truth means. True worshipers love God and live in love with their neighbors. False worshipers bring offerings with morally unclean hands. When Jesus said that God was seeking worshipers who worshiped in truth, He was almost certainly describing whether or not we worship God with pure motives and clean lives. In other words, God wants true worship, without phoniness.

If we were to look for true worshipers, what would we expect to find? The Spirit's work always will result in lives characterized by love. "God has poured out his love into our hearts by the Holy Spirit, whom he has given us" (Romans 5:5). Therefore, we should love others by the Spirit (Romans 15:30; Colossians 1:8). In addition to love, Paul said that the fruit of the Spirit's work in our lives will bring about character transformation in us. "The fruit of the Spirit is love, joy, peace, patience, kindness, goodness, faithfulness, gentleness and self-control. Against such things there is no law" (Galatians 5:22-23). People who are true in their offerings are people who bear the fruit of His work. We know God has been among us because we are walking in and demonstrating love, joy, peace, patience, kindness, goodness, faithfulness, gentleness and self-control.

Many Christians rejoice that God has set them free from the confines of Old Testament worship—the temple gone, the burnt offerings forgotten, the temple choir long silent. Now the Spirit Himself sanctifies each believer as an offering to God, transforming broken lives to sweet-smelling savors to God. We, on our part, must be true sacrifices, offering ourselves without wrath and dissention (1 Timothy 2:8).

QUESTION:
How do I worship in spirit and truth?

PRINCIPLE **22**

C. I worship in truth when the Holy Spirit's fruit (love, joy, peace, patience, kindness, goodness, faithfulness, gentleness and self-control) accompanies my worship.

● ● ●

Jeff explained what he had found in the Scriptures concerning worshiping in spirit and truth. Charles still found the verse confusing. At this point in his life, however, nothing surprised him. Finally, he asked the question that bothered him the most.

"Pastor, are you saying that singing and praising God isn't worship?"

Jeff smiled. "No, Charles, I'm not saying that. But I am saying that you can't assume that you can tell that the Holy Spirit is working among us by what you feel."

Charles leaned back and thought for a moment. "You used to teach us that when we praised God with joy He dwelt among us in a powerful way."

Nodding, Jeff paused for a moment and then answered. "I know, but every time I have studied this verse in the past two weeks, I have realized how weak my understanding of worship really was. Now, I think that sometimes God does give us emotional excitement. Other times He doesn't. Both show us that He is working."

Jeff's answer confused Charles. If the pastor was right, then worship would be so much different from what Charles had always understood.

Then suddenly it hit him. Charles had been studying the Psalms and finding out that worship for David was much different than it had been for himself. David brought all of his life to God when he sang to Him, bringing complaints even more than he offered praises. Worship in the Old Testament did appeal more to Israel's senses, but David's worship songs covered all of life, including God's silence and His discipline.

When Charles described what he had been learning, Jeff saw worship in a new light. Worship was not about happiness and excitement, but was about bringing our lives to God. That's what Charles was learning from the Psalms, and it made sense. Worship began with loving God with all of our heart, soul, mind and strength, not just with our happy singing. God wants us to be real before Him in our worship, and that's what Jeff wanted to bring into First Community Church's worship.

They were on the verge of a new understanding. God was surely working among them.

TEN

What Forms Do I Use to Bring My Worship to God . . . ?

QUESTION:
What forms do I use to bring my
worship to God, now that the temple,
priests and sacrifices have passed away?

PRINCIPLE 12:

A: All Christians are now priests who bring sacrifices
and offerings to God.

B: Both individual believers and believers as a whole
are the temple where offerings and sacrifices are
brought to God.

C: I present my life in service to others as a living sacrifice and offering to God.

Fred and Janice's house, Saturday morning, March 10

Janice looked in on Fred again. He had been sitting in his chair all morning, doing nothing. All week Fred had been doing the same thing, coming home, eating dinner and then just sitting in his chair. Janice asked him once what he was doing and the only answer she received was, "Thinking."

Fred's "thinking" could not go on forever. The grass needed mowing and Fred had chores. Besides, she was getting worried. He had never done this before.

"Fred?"

Silence.

"Fred, I need you to help me."

Fred looked up. "Help with what?"

Silently praying, Janice answered, "Fred, I'm worried about you. All you've done the past five days is just sit there. What's going on? You're scaring me."

Fred sighed. If he said it out loud, he would have to face it and deal with it. But she was right—he couldn't sit here forever. He made up his mind and spoke.

"I was wrong about Pastor Rick. I know that I was wrong. I can't get away from it."

Janice sat down across from her husband. She had guessed that Rick was the problem, but did not expect Fred to own up to it.

He continued. "I know that I have to do something about it, but I don't want to. If I go to Rick and ask his forgiveness, then it means that everything that happened at church was my fault. I destroyed Rick and his wife, chased away about a quarter of our members and made everyone miserable."

Her husband's words stunned her. That would mean that she contributed to the whole mess too. Janice did not want to think about that.

"Honey," she replied, "Rick came to our church without caring about us and our feelings at all. He . . ."

"No," Fred interrupted, "it doesn't matter what Rick did. I need to deal with what *I* did. I stabbed Rick in the back and now everything is messed up."

Janice knew that was true. Fred had stopped at nothing to remove Pastor Rick from First Community.

She looked nervously at her husband. "So, what are you planning on doing?"

Fred sighed again. "Planning? I'm not planning anything. But I think I need to ask the pastor to go with me to see Rick."

Janice felt a twinge of fear run through her. She had no intention of apologizing to Rick. He had caused a lot of problems at their church. Of course, he had paid dearly for his sins. And she and Fred had been very hurtful toward him.

Finally, Fred spoke again. "Look, Janice, you may not agree with me, but if I don't get this off my chest, I'm not going to be able to get out of this chair. Could you get me the phone and the church number?"

*   *   *

Once Fred repented of his sin before God, what was he to do next? The Bible does not require that he do penance. Jesus paid the price for Fred's sins. Sadly, others had paid a price for Fred's sins as well. He might not be able to undo the damage he had done to them.

Yet Fred still could present an offering of worship to Jesus, who had cleansed him. Obviously, he would not slay a ram or bring a grain offering to church. His offering to God would be something far more meaningful. It would happen when he gave up his life as a sacrifice to heal those whom he had so badly wounded.

Jesus was the true Sacrifice, the true Temple, the true Passover—He was everything. The New Testament does not command God's people to bring animal sacrifices to a new Christian temple. Yet Peter and Paul often talked about the temple, priests and presenting God with offerings and sacrifices (1 Corinthians 3:16-17; Ephesians 2:21; 1 Peter 2:1-10). If we no longer present offerings to priests in a holy temple, why did these two writers use these words so often?

Answering that question opens up a whole new side to worship. Christians still have a temple, priests, offerings and sacrifices. This reality brings a remarkable fullness to what the Bible says worship is for the church today.

The New Priesthood

The priests of Israel were unique among the people. Only a small portion of the Israelites could serve as priests, those who were from the tribe of Levi and descended from Aaron. Priests were anointed with a perfumed oil, so that they carried about them the aroma of holiness. God permitted priests alone to approach the temple altar. He permitted priests alone to offer incense before Himself. He permitted priests alone to enter the holy place. The Law set the priests apart as a unique group within Israel.

At Pentecost, a remarkable transformation occurred in the concept of the priesthood. Until then, only a small portion of Israel could serve as priests. Now, all who are born of the Spirit through faith in Jesus Christ have been set apart as priests. The book of Revelation tells us that Christ "loves us and has freed us from our sins by his blood, and has made us to be a kingdom and priests to serve his God and Father—to him be glory and power for ever and ever! Amen" (Revelation 1:5-6). Christians are priests for the world. The lost meet God through believers, who bring Christ to the world and the world to Christ. Peter exhorted Christians to offer spiritual sacrifices: "You also, like living stones, are being built into a spiritual house to be a holy priesthood, offering spiritual sacrifices acceptable to God through Jesus Christ" (1 Peter 2:5).

As a holy priesthood, we are to offer spiritual sacrifices to God. Before we can fully understand what Peter meant by this, however, we must first understand why he called us a "spiritual house."

QUESTION:
What forms do I use to bring my worship to
God, now that the temple, priests
and sacrifices have passed away?

PRINCIPLE 12:

A: All Christians are now priests who bring sacrifices and offerings to God.

The New Temple

The church is a spiritual house where priests offer sacrifices to God. In his writings, the Apostle Paul several times described the church as a temple. "Don't you know that you yourselves are God's temple and that God's Spirit lives in you? If anyone destroys God's temple, God will destroy him; for God's temple is sacred, and you are that temple" (1 Corinthians 3:16-17). Paul also taught that the church is a "building [that is] joined together and rises to become a holy temple in the Lord. And in him you too are being built together to become a dwelling in which God lives by his Spirit" (Ephesians 2:21-22).

When Jesus was on earth, He was the New Temple, where humankind could meet with God. In this study we have discovered that the old temple's main function was to be the central place of sacrifice and offerings for Israel. Jesus was not only the New Temple, but He also was the final Sacrifice for sin.

After Jesus ascended to the Father, the Father and Son sent the Spirit into the Church at Pentecost. That day, flames of fire descended upon those individuals in the upper room, similar to the way God's glory filled the temple when it was dedicated. "They saw what seemed to be tongues of fire that separated and came to rest on each of them. All of them were filled with the Holy Spirit and began to speak in other tongues as the Spirit enabled them" (Acts 2:3-4). The flames of fire separated and came to rest upon each person there, man and woman alike. Just as the glory of God had descended upon the tabernacle when Moses dedicated it and upon the temple when Solomon finished it, so God's glory descended upon the church at Pentecost.

But the church serves as a temple in a way different from Solomon's or Herod's temple. Until Jesus, worshipers could offer sacrifices only in Jerusalem. When the Holy Spirit descended upon the Church, the New Temple left Jerusalem to reach to the ends of the earth. Now, God does not dwell in Jerusalem alone, but in the lives of true believers everywhere. The world comes to the New

Temple, the Church, to find forgiveness for sin through Christ.

> But thanks be to God, who always leads us in triumphal procession in Christ and through us spreads everywhere the fragrance of the knowledge of him. For we are to God the aroma of Christ among those who are being saved and those who are perishing. To the one we are the smell of death; to the other, the fragrance of life. And who is equal to such a task? (2 Corinthians 2:14-16)

So, the New Testament teaches that Christians are both the priests of the world and the New Temple in the world. Peter also taught that we are to bring sacrifices in this spiritual temple, but what kind of sacrifices do we offer as priests to the world?

QUESTION:
What forms do I use to bring my worship
to God, now that the temple,
priests and sacrifices have passed away?

PRINCIPLE 12:

B: Both individual believers and believers as a whole are the New Temple where sacrifices and offerings are brought to God.

Living Sacrifices

In Romans 12:1, Paul exhorted his readers to give themselves to God as a *thusia,* the word used by the Septuagint (the ancient Greek translation of the Old Testament often used by Paul's readers) to translate *minhah*. "Therefore, I urge you, brothers, in view of God's mercy, to offer your bodies as living sacrifices, holy and pleasing to God—this is your spiritual act of worship." Remember that Jews offered a *minhah* as a way to present themselves to God, asking Him to accept them as His servants. Paul described this offering as their "spiritual act of worship" (the Greek word *latreuo*). The word *worship* is the word the Septuagint uses to translate *abad*, the Hebrew word for religious service to God. We already have seen that *abad* describes serving God by bringing offerings and sacrifices. Remarkably, Paul said that by presenting ourselves to God, we are doing our *abad*, our religious services of worship.

What did Paul mean when he commanded believers to present themselves as *thusia* sacrifices to God? We must read the rest of Romans 12 to understand the answer. Paul said that we must allow our minds to be transformed so that we might prove what is the will of God, which is serving one another. In addition, we must not think too highly of ourselves (12:3); we must minister according to our gifts (12:6-8); and our love must be without hypocrisy (12:9-21). All of these activities center on serving others. Paul seems to suggest that the Christian who serves his brother is indeed offering *thusia* offerings to God.

Whenever you find Paul using the terms *thusia* and *latreuo*, he is describing service to others. These two words, which in the Greek translation of the Old Testament describe bringing offerings and sacrifices to God, in the New Testament describe ministering to those in need. For example, Paul told the Romans that he served (Greek *latreuo,* translating *abad*) God; that is, he did his religious service to God through the preaching of the gospel. "God, whom I serve with my whole heart in preaching the gospel of his Son, is my witness how constantly I remember you" (Romans 1:9). He also served (*latreuo*) God in his prayers: "I thank God, whom I serve, as my forefathers did, with a clear conscience, as night and day I constantly remember you in my prayers" (2 Timothy 1:3). Paul's prayer ministry for Timothy was *latreia*. His preaching of the gospel also was *latreia* (the noun form of the word *latreuo*).

Paul told the Philippians that if he were to die in Rome, his martyrdom would be a religious offering that he could present to God. "But even if I am being poured out like a drink offering on the sacrifice (*thusia*) and service coming from your faith, I am glad and rejoice with all of you" (Philippians 2:17). Paul's death would be the same as bringing a sacrifice or offering to the temple, but his life was the offering He presented to God in worship.

Paul used another Greek word for worship offerings, *prosphora*, to describe his ministry to the Gentiles.

> I have written you quite boldly on some points, as if to remind you of them again, because of the grace God gave me to be a minister of Christ Jesus to the Gentiles with the priestly duty of proclaiming the gospel of God, so that the Gentiles might become an offering acceptable to God, sanctified by the Holy Spirit. (Romans 15:15-16)

The apostle likened himself to a priest who presents to God an offering (*prosphora*). What was his offering? The people who came to Christ through his preaching of the gospel. This sounds much like First Peter 2:9: "But you are a chosen people, a royal priesthood, a holy nation, a people belonging to God, that you may declare the praises of him who called you out of darkness into his wonderful light." Christians are the priests of the world. God has chosen us to be His tool through whom the sacrifice of His Son is made effective by the Church's preaching of the gospel. When we give our lives to bring the gospel to others, we are presenting to God an offering of worship.

The apostle wrote these passages using Old Testament sacrificial language. He purposely wanted the Philippians to see that their true sacrifices to God, their true temple service to their Savior, was through ministry to others. The Philippians had sent Paul a rich gift to supply his needs. This gift was a *thusia*, pleasing to God. "I have received full payment and even more; I am amply supplied, now that I have received from Epaphroditus the gifts you sent. They are a fragrant offering, an acceptable sacrifice, pleasing to God" (Philippians 4:18). Paul's life was an offering; the Philippians' generosity was an offering; preaching the gospel was an offering; prayer for Timothy was an offering. It's the same for us today. Giving up one's life for others is an offering; serving the body of Christ is an offering. All Christians are priests like Paul, who present their service and sacrifice to God as offerings of worship.

If we were to apply Peter and Paul's theology to worship, we would transform the Church. All Christians are priests. All Christians are temples, both corporately and individually. Believers now carry out their religious worship to God through serving other people. It is as we surrender our rights for others and pour out our lives for others that we minister our worship unto God. The Sunday morning service may be a time for praise and thanksgiving, but our songs and praises are not our *minhah* offerings nor our *'ola* offerings. Our true offerings of worship are when we present our bodies as a living sacrifice in ministry to others.

Even Hebrews 13:15-16 teaches us that our true offerings of worship are not our words but our lives. "Through Jesus, therefore, let us continually offer to God a sacrifice of praise—the fruit of lips that confess his name. And do not forget to do good and to share with others, for with such sacrifices God is pleased." The word *confess* is very important to the book of Hebrews. The readers feared persecution and were considering denying Christ and returning to Judaism. So the author of Hebrews urged them to reconsider, to offer to God a sacrifice of praise. Their praise sacrifice was that they would courageously confess Christ's name even if it meant persecution. That would be their real sacrifice to God. In addition, they were to present to God another offering of worship—doing good and sharing with others. They would not bring their sacrifice of praises through their songs but through their confession and service to others.

This fits very well into the Old Testament's approach to worship. Right from the beginning, God cared more about the heart than the offering. The *'ola* was important because it pictured Jesus Christ as our atoning Sacrifice. The *minhah* was important because it made a statement to God that the worshiper saw Him as Lord and Master and himself as servant. Nevertheless, neither offering had any impact unless the worshiper's heart was right. Most often, the prophets judged the purity of the Israelites' hearts by how they treated the poor, the needy, the orphans and the widows. Peter and Paul applied these truths to the New Temple, which is the Church. The new sacrifice, our own lives, is not entirely new. The prophets already proclaimed it. And James wrote, "Religion that God our Father accepts as pure and faultless is this: to look after orphans and widows in their distress and to keep oneself from being polluted by the world" (James 1:27).

In our story, Fred is about to offer God a sacrifice of worship. He is about to go to Pastor Rick, because Rick needs healing that only Fred can offer. Fred is going to suffer when he does this, yet the suffering is not his worship. What he does for Rick on his behalf will be worship. Fred is the priest and the temple, and his life is the offering. In order for Fred to come to this point, he had to transform his mind, to not think more highly of himself than he ought to think, and to love Rick. This is how Christians present to God their offerings of worship.

QUESTION:
What forms do I use to bring my worship
to God, now that the temple,
priests and sacrifices have passed away?

PRINCIPLE 12:

C: I present my own life in service to others as a living sacrifice and offering to God.

The Shadow of the Cross

Why would God command us to present ourselves as living sacrifices? Has God not called us to enjoy blessing? After all, Peter wrote, "To this you were called so that you may inherit a blessing" (1 Peter 3:9). Indeed, God has called us to blessing, the blessing of being like Jesus Christ, who came to die for the sins of the world. Jesus began His announcement of the kingdom by teaching that blessing comes to us in spiritual poverty, mourning, hungering and thirsting, and persecution (Matthew 5:3-12). How could such things bring blessing to us? They bless us when they transform us from being people who seek pleasure and satisfaction to those who seek to be like Jesus. When we die for the sake of our brothers and sisters and for the sake of the lost, we become more and more like Jesus. "To this you were called, because Christ suffered for you, leaving you an example, that you should follow in his steps" (1 Peter 2:21).

God does not call us to suffer because He is "out to get us." He wants to transform us to be like His Son. To be like Jesus is to die as Jesus died, for the sake of others. "For even the Son of Man did not come to be served, but to serve, and to give his life as a ransom for many" (Mark 10:45). Do you want to be like Jesus? He came to earth carrying a cross to die for the sins of the world. We too must bear His cross. "Then he called the crowd to him along with his disciples and said: 'If anyone would come after me, he must deny himself and take up his cross and follow me. For whoever wants to save his life will lose it, but whoever loses his life for me and for the gospel will save it' " (8:34-35). Notice that we lose our lives for Jesus' sake *and for the sake of the gospel*. To be like Jesus, we must die as Jesus died—for the sake of the gospel.

For worship to be true worship, it must reflect the shadow of the cross in our lives. We take up our crosses and follow Jesus, presenting ourselves as living sacrifices for the sake of others. When we bear His cross, we look like Him. When others see us, they see beyond our sacrifices to the true sacrifice of the Lamb of God. As we bear Christ's cross, we reflect the heart of the gospel to the world. Our lives say, "See Christ's death in my death for you. I love you because Jesus loves you."

*   *   *

On the way to Pastor Rick's home, Saturday afternoon, March 10

Pastor Jeff turned the corner and pulled into Rick and Jeri's driveway. Fred had remained silent the entire trip. Jeff could tell that he was dreading this meeting.

He turned off the car and looked at Fred. "Well, Fred, are you ready?"

Fred slowly nodded. "Pastor, will you pray for me the whole time I'm talking?"

"I promise you I won't stop praying."

Reaching for the car door, Fred added, "I guess you'd better pray more for Pastor Rick than for me. It's going to take a lot of healing to fix what I've done to him."

They both got out and walked slowly to the house. Before they could even knock, Jeri had already opened the door. "Come on in Pastor, Fred. We've been waiting for you."

How Can I Experience God's Glory in My Worship?

P R I N C I P L E 1 3 :

God exposes His glory most completely when in weakness I die to myself, offering up my rights and comfort for the sake of others.

Choir prayer meeting, Saturday evening, March 10

Eleven people crowded into the living room. Isabelle could see on their faces how committed they were becoming to this prayer meeting. Charles and Sharlene sat on the floor, hand in hand, their presence an answer to prayer in itself. Above the chatter Isabelle heard the doorbell. A few moments later, Troy appeared in the hallway with Fred. As they entered the room, the group quieted, all eyes focused on Fred.

Fred stood in the doorway while Troy called the time to order. "As usual, we're here to pray for what's happening tomorrow in church. But I was wondering if anyone has anything to say."

Clearing his throat, Fred nervously began to speak. "Yeah, Troy, I need to say something."

He paused and looked around the room. "I . . . just got back from talking to Pastor Rick and Jeri about an hour ago." He looked down again. "Guess I've really destroyed their lives. Our meeting was pretty rough. Pastor Jeff was there to keep things from getting ugly, but, well, it was pretty ugly anyway."

Fred's words caught Isabelle entirely off guard. His arrival that evening had surprised her enough, but to think that Fred had gone to see Pastor Rick defied imagination. What happened next went even beyond that.

Charles stood up and walked over to where Fred was standing. He reached out to shake Fred's hand. Fred looked surprised.

"I just want to say," Charles began, "that I have been doing a lot of thinking in the past few weeks. I've hurt our church by the way I totally ignored your feelings about different kinds of music. I'm sorry."

He paused, looking Fred in the eye. "And Fred, I'll be honest. I hated you. You were in my way and I wanted to get rid of you."

Isabelle could see that Fred understood what Charles was saying, because he nodded and grasped hold of his hand to shake it. She didn't quite understand all that was happening, but her eyes were brimming with tears.

Fred glanced around the room and began to speak again. "You people have really suffered through this whole nasty thing. I lied about some things. I . . . um . . . manipulated the board to do things it otherwise would never have done. I'm really sorry, everyone. I'm just really sorry."

Troy asked Charles and Fred to sit down and then suggested they spend the rest of the evening in prayer.

Who can explain what happens when the Holy Spirit takes over a prayer meeting? For two and a half hours, they gave thanks for God's love and offered prayers that Pastor Rick would find healing. There was nothing fancy about the meeting that night, nothing showy, nothing amazing. Yet more than Isabelle could ever remember, she saw the glory of God poured out over those who were praying. It was not a glory of miracles. It was the glory of His love.

*   *   *

When Isabelle thought she saw God's glory in that prayer meeting, she was not looking at the kind of brilliant glow of glory that shone in Moses' face during Israel's days in the wilderness. Moses' glory came when he entered the tent of meeting, surrounded by God's presence. When he left that place, his face shone so brightly that the Israelites begged him to cover it so that they would not have to look upon God's glory (Exodus 34:29-35). Isabelle was gazing on a different kind of glory. That evening the glory of the cross shone brightly in the prayer group's midst.

In the Old Testament, God's glory was an awesome and terrifying presence. When it fell upon the original temple nobody dared even approach it. The New Temple, which consists of all those who belong to Jesus Christ, seems so dramatically different from the glorious temple in Jerusalem. The original temple was a building of astonishing beauty and holiness. Worshipers surely were aware of its holiness and awe as they approached the steps and inhaled the odor of burnt offerings. When the priests walked by, the tiny bells on the rims of their robes and the aroma of anointing perfumes gave believers a sense of sacredness and wonder. Believers today, however, do not seem so awesome, so fearful, so wondrous.

Christ's Cross Is Our Glory

Yet in Paul's theology (and in Jesus' as well), the glory that flows from believers far surpasses the glory of the Old Testament tabernacle or temple. Indeed, there still is a holy aroma to the New Temple of God.

> But thanks be to God, who always leads us in triumphal procession in Christ and through us spreads everywhere the fragrance of the knowledge of him. For we are to God the aroma of Christ among those who are being saved and those who are perishing. To the one we are the smell of death; to the other, the fragrance of life. And who is equal to such a task? (2 Corinthians 2:14-16)

The aroma that goes out from us either draws people to Christ or utterly repels them.

Many aspects of the Old Testament temple were specifically designed to communicate a sense of God's glory, but how is that done through the New Temple? Paul developed a remarkable answer in Second Corinthians 3-5.

Moses' glory was external. First, we must understand that the glory that filled the tabernacle/temple was a temporary and external glory. Moses regularly came in contact with that glory. His face was so bright that it drove the people to beg him to wear a veil. Notice that this glory was external to Moses. He soaked it in, so to speak, when he stood in God's presence. After a while, the glory in Moses' face would fade until he would return to the tent of meeting to speak with the Lord.

Our glory comes from the Holy Spirit within us.

> Even to this day when Moses is read, a veil covers their hearts. But whenever anyone turns to the Lord, the veil is taken away. Now the Lord is the Spirit, and where the Spirit of the Lord is, there is freedom. And we, who with unveiled faces all reflect the Lord's glory, are being transformed into his likeness with ever-increasing glory, which comes from the Lord, who is the Spirit. (3:15-18)

Three significant aspects of the temple are clearly fulfilled in the Church. First, the body of Christ, like the temple before it, is the dwelling place of God. Second, all believers, like the temple before them, have an aroma that reveals Christ's sacrifice for sin. Third, God's glory shines through the Church just as it did through the temple.

Our glory comes through our suffering for others. But wait. Where do we see glory shining from the Church today? Is it in our marvelous buildings? Do our perfectly orchestrated worship services reveal glory? Perhaps the architects of the great cathedrals of Europe were right after all: We must create an atmosphere of glory to match the glory of the Old Testament temple.

Paul, however, contradicted all of those ideas of glory. The glory that the Church must exude is the light of Christ. "For we do not preach ourselves, but Jesus Christ as Lord, and ourselves as your servants for Jesus' sake. For God, who said, 'Let light shine out of darkness,' made his light shine in our hearts to give us the light of the knowledge of the glory of God in the face of Christ" (4:5-6).

How then is that light released to reveal Christ? Paul said that God exposes the light through our suffering for the sake of Christ.

> But we have this treasure in jars of clay to show that this all-surpassing power is from God and not from us. We are hard pressed on every side, but not crushed; perplexed, but not in despair; persecuted, but not abandoned; struck down, but not destroyed. We always carry around in our body the death of Jesus, so that the life of Jesus may also be revealed in our body. For we who are alive are always being given over to death for Jesus' sake, so that his life may be revealed in our mortal body. So then, death is at work in us, but life is at work in you. (4:7-12)

The glory of Christ is revealed as we suffer for Christ. When Fred struggled with Pastor Rick's music ministry, he rejected the call to suffer. For Fred, if the worship service was unpleasant, he simply refused to experience it. He wanted the service to bless him, but he did not understand what true blessing meant. Jesus,

Peter, Paul and the writer of Hebrews taught that the real blessings of life in this age are eternal. Sometimes those blessings hurt. For example, the greatest blessing in life is to be like Jesus Himself. We become like Jesus when we love others. "This is how we know what love is: Jesus Christ laid down his life for us. And we ought to lay down our lives for our brothers" (1 John 3:16). Yet we must take up Jesus' cross if we are to love the way He loved, which brings us into profound pain. Fred did not want to accept God's gift of pain.

The blessing of being like Jesus often comes to us in the form of suffering. Jesus promised us blessings, but they are far from pleasant.

> Blessed are you who are poor,
>   for yours is the kingdom of God.
> Blessed are you who hunger now,
>   for you will be satisfied.
> Blessed are you who weep now,
>   for you will laugh. (Luke 6:20-21)

Jesus did not teach that pain itself is the blessing. Instead, the blessing comes wrapped up in suffering as we learn to exchange the pleasures of this world for the treasures of heaven. Until the resurrection, God uses our suffering as a furnace to refine our faith until it shines like gold.

> In this you greatly rejoice, though now for a little while you may have had to suffer grief in all kinds of trials. These have come so that your faith—of greater worth than gold, which perishes even though refined by fire—may be proved genuine and may result in

praise, glory and honor when Jesus Christ is revealed. (1 Peter 1:6-7)

Paul specifically described suffering in terms of his
sacrificial ministries for the churches. As the apostles
and missionaries underwent persecution, perplexity
and affliction so that others could live, God's glory was
revealed. Only then was the power clearly seen as God's
and not as man's. Suffering revealed glory and also produced a greater and greater promise of eternal glory.

> Therefore we do not lose heart. Though outwardly
> we are wasting away, yet inwardly we are being re-
> newed day by day. For our light and momentary trou-
> bles are achieving for us an eternal glory that far
> outweighs them all. So we fix our eyes not on what is
> seen, but on what is unseen. For what is seen is tempo-
> rary, but what is unseen is eternal. (2 Corinthians
> 4:16-18)

Perhaps in our story Sharlene most showed that kind
of glory. The suffering she experienced as she watched
her son die revealed God's love to her most clearly. As
Sharlene suffered, however, she began to know Jesus in
a way she had never known Him before. The pain was
not the glory, yet the glory would not have come without it.

Several months ago I sat and talked with a man who
had been through horrible suffering over the past year.
Yet he told me that those months brought him the
deepest joy he had ever known. It was a painful joy, to
be sure. He told me that it was not at all a happy joy.
The look on his face, however, made me realize how

deep it was. The joy he knew through such profound suffering revealed the glory of Christ's cross.

Our glory reflects the cross. The temple gave Israel a picture of the Christ to come. When Jesus came to us, God shrouded His glory with suffering. The angels gloriously proclaimed His birth to the shepherds, singing, "Glory to God in the highest, and on earth peace to men on whom his favor rests" (Luke 2:14). Yet the shepherds found Messiah's glory hidden in a stable, lying in a feeding trough, surrounded by poverty and humiliation, wrapped in strips of cloth. Later on as a man, that same Son of God revealed His glory as He walked among His people. He had no place to lay His head as He lived and served sinners. His glory shone most brightly in the places of greatest darkness. Jesus denied Himself the blessings of heaven that He might bring those blessings to sinful humankind.

Surely in the history of creation, God's glory never shone so brightly as it did the day Jesus died on Golgotha. What a gruesome spectacle of glory, when the broken, suffering, defeated Savior bore the sins of the world. Those who look for brilliant flashes of glory do not stay long upon that hill. Yet those who yearn to know God would do well to gaze at the gashes on His back to understand His glory. See the thorns pierce His forehead to comprehend His greatness. Hear His gasping breath to grasp the depths of His love for us.

As He cries out, *"Eloi, Eloi, lama sabachthani?"* (My God, my God, why have you forsaken me?—Matthew 27:46), God's glory overwhelms those who long to know Him. The searching heart cannot plunge these depths of glory, of God crushing His Son to save sinners from death. The brightness of the Mount of Transfiguration pales next to the darkness of Golgotha. Jesus told us it would be so:

> The hour has come for the Son of Man to be glorified. I tell you the truth, unless a kernel of wheat falls to the ground and dies, it remains only a single seed. But if it dies, it produces many seeds. The man who loves his life will lose it, while the man who hates his life in this world will keep it for eternal life. (John 12:23-25)

God's greatest glory shone through the darkest cross, when Jesus, God's only Son, died for the sins of the world.

Doesn't it make sense that if Christ's death on our behalf is the greatest revelation of God's glory, then our deaths on behalf of others also would be a revelation of God's glory? Indeed, how can we reveal Christ any more clearly than through suffering for the sake of others? Paul clearly teaches in Second Corinthians that God's glory is most truly exposed when we die for those who need Christ's love and ministry. Christians must be like Christ, no longer living for themselves but for the sake of others.

> We are not trying to commend ourselves to you again, but are giving you an opportunity to take pride in us, so that you can answer those who take pride in what is seen rather than in what is in the heart. If we are out of our mind, it is for the sake of God; if we are in our right mind, it is for you. For Christ's love compels us, because we are convinced that one died for all, and therefore all died. And he died for all, that those who live should no longer live for themselves but for him who died for them and was raised again. (2 Corinthians 5:12-15)

The old glory was not really glory at all.

QUESTION:
How can I experience God's glory in my worship?

PRINCIPLE 13:

God exposes His glory most completely when in weakness I die to myself, offering up my rights and comfort for the sake of others.

---

* * *

Troy closed the front door after Fred drove away. He sat down on the couch next to Isabelle, who seemed to be asleep.

"Who would have thought . . . ," she said with her eyes still closed.

Troy looked up. "Who would have thought what?"

"Who would have thought," she continued, "that we would be able to help those two reconcile?"

Her husband smiled. "How in the world did we help? Jeff's the one who took Fred over to see Rick."

Isabelle put her arms around her husband. "No, Troy Smith. You are the one who asked Fred to fix your lawnmower when you didn't want to. You are the one who invited Fred and Janice over for dinner."

"It's an amazing thing, isn't it?" Troy replied. "Seeing the impossible happen right before your eyes?"

She nodded and smiled. "The most amazing miracles are sometimes the ones we barely see."

"Yep," Troy answered, "that's what Jesus is all about, isn't He?"

TWELVE

How Does God Want Christians to Worship Together?

QUESTION:
How does God want Christians to worship together?

PRINCIPLE 14:

Everything we do in corporate worship should build up fellow believers. We should sing and speak truth to their minds so that they will grow in their understanding of God and learn to live in godliness.

Choir prayer meeting, Saturday evening, June 2

Marcia looked around the room. "I'm more nervous about tomorrow than I've ever been about a church service. Bringing music back into our services scares me."

Several people around the room nodded in agreement.

Andrea spoke up. "How can we make sure that the same kind of disaster won't happen again, Troy?"

All eyes focused on Troy, who smiled. "Well, first of all, I think that we need to keep on praying every week. God has done more here through this prayer meeting than anywhere else I know of in our church."

Nobody seemed to disagree with that.

"Also, the pastor and I have worked hard on our music for tomorrow," he continued. "We only chose songs that we felt have a real message."

Donna looked somewhat confused. "What do you mean, 'a message'?"

He opened the folder on his lap and handed out bulletins for the Sunday service. "We've prayed about each song. If we can ask God to use the song to do something constructive in people's lives, then we feel its message is important."

Everyone looked at the bulletin for Sunday's service. Both hymns and choruses were included.

"Now," said Troy, "it's time to pray. We need to pray for our people that God will do a great work in their lives through each chorus and hymn. Pray that the words will help them grow in their walk with Christ. Pray that they will know God better because of the words."

As they prepared to pray, Marcia spoke up. "This is so different from the way we used to approach our worship time. I used to pray that God would bless us through the music. Now it sounds like you're saying that we should pray that He will use these songs to change us."

"And He will," Charles added. "Trust me—there's no greater blessing than being changed by God."

They began to pray.

* * *

The choir members were discovering what many others have found over the years. If you do not know what to pray that a song or hymn will accomplish during a church service, that song or hymn probably cannot accomplish much of anything. This was, perhaps, the greatest problem with music in First Community Church before Troy came. People were judging the value of the choruses and hymns they sang on the type of music they used. But the real issue should have been the message of the songs.

Of course, most people did not recognize the real problem. Those who were more conservative, for instance, might have criticized choruses for being shallow in content. Yet they probably sang hymns and gospel choruses on a regular basis that were every bit as trivial. Neither side could understand how to bring reconciliation because both sides had missed the real point of singing songs in corporate worship.

We Worship to Build Up Others

Ephesians 5:18-20 tells us,

> Do not get drunk on wine, which leads to debauchery. Instead, be filled with the Spirit. Speak to one another with psalms, hymns and spiritual songs. Sing and make music in your heart to the Lord, always giving thanks to God the Father for everything, in the name of our Lord Jesus Christ.

Why should we worry about speaking to one another through our psalms, hymns and spiritual songs when we are supposed to be worshiping? Shouldn't God be the focus of worship? If we make one another as much the focus of our worship as God, our worship will become human-centered rather than God-centered, which seems to contradict the idea of worship.

Paul answered this question for us in his letter to the Colossians.

> Let the word of Christ richly dwell within you, with all wisdom *teaching* [Greek *didasko*] and *admonishing* [Greek *noutheteo*] one another with psalms and hymns and spiritual songs, singing with thankfulness in your hearts to God. And whatever you do in word or deed, do all in the name of the Lord Jesus, giving thanks through Him to God the Father. (Colossians 3:16-17, NASB)

When we gather together in corporate worship, we are to use praise and worship songs as a means of teaching and admonishing one another.

These two words are significant in Paul's epistles. When Paul used the word for "teaching" (Greek *didasko*), he almost always was describing teaching doctrine or Christian truth. He especially used this word in his letters to Timothy and Titus, where the purity and teaching of godly doctrine dominates much of those epistles. The word for "admonishing" (Greek *noutheteo*) has the idea "to provide instruction as to correct behavior and belief—'to instruct, to teach, instruction, teaching.' "[1] *Noutheteo* focuses on behavior and attitude change. This suggests when Christians gather together to worship, their worship should focus on instructing one another in good doctrine and godly behavior. Worship is a time of spiritual formation and development. Paul wrote that what would normally be seen as only vertical activities (worship toward God alone) should be viewed as horizontal activities as well, so that they convey information and admonition to those who listen. Thus, Paul's instruction to "speak to one another with psalms, hymns and spiritual songs" is a command to teach doctrine and stir one another on to good works.

In the church, we are to conduct our worship time with a view toward edifying each other. Clearly, there is a vertical view to worship as well, since we are to sing and make music in our hearts to the Lord. Corporate worship is incomplete unless we incorporate both dimensions, so that we are building up one another and also praising and thanking God.

If the people praying at Troy's house wanted to know how to ask God to use each song in the service, they would need to follow Paul's instructions in Ephesians 5—that is, pray that the songs would edify the congregation. What, however, does the word *edify* mean?

Edification: Speaking Truth to the Mind

Paul defined edification in First Corinthians 14. Apparently many people in the congregation at Corinth had been speaking in uninterpreted tongues in their times of corporate worship. Paul explained that this was not the correct way to go about worship.

> Now, brothers, if I come to you and speak in tongues, what good will I be to you, unless I bring you some revelation or knowledge or prophecy or word of instruction? Even in the case of lifeless

things that make sounds, such as the flute or harp, how will anyone know what tune is being played unless there is a distinction in the notes? Again, if the trumpet does not sound a clear call, who will get ready for battle? So it is with you. Unless you speak intelligible words with your tongue, how will anyone know what you are saying? You will just be speaking into the air. Undoubtedly there are all sorts of languages in the world, yet none of them is without meaning. If then I do not grasp the meaning of what someone is saying, I am a foreigner to the speaker, and he is a foreigner to me. (1 Corinthians 14:6-11)

There was no point in speaking in tongues without interpretation, because those who listened could not understand. If they did not understand, they could not grow. "So it is with you," Paul continued. "Since you are eager to have spiritual gifts, try to excel in gifts that *build up the church*" (14:12). When we are worshiping in a church setting, we should always seek to build up others.

Notice that Paul said edification can occur only when the mind is instructed. An electric thrill may run through the congregation as everyone begins to speak in tongues, but this thrill is not edification. People are edified only when words are spoken to their minds, so that they can think about these words and be transformed by them.

My students often argue against this principle. They disagree that when people speak in tongues during worship, they cannot edify others unless those who hear understand with their minds what has been said. My students contend that even though there are no distinct words, people are built up in their faith. I tell them not to take my word for it, but Paul's: "If I come to you and speak in tongues, *what good will I be to you,* unless I bring you some *revelation* or *knowledge* or *prophecy* or *word of instruction?*" (14:6). Words must be spoken *to the mind* for edification to happen. That is the message of First Corinthians 14. Paul wanted the Corinthians to judge everything that went on in corporate worship by whether or not it built up the body of Christ. This fits what we have already seen about faith. Faith needs information, not emotion. Thus, everything we do in a worship service must speak to the mind.

Does this include prayer, usually a private practice? During corporate worship, we might assume that prayer would still be considered personal. Paul, however, said that those who pray in the congregation must seek to edify the other members through the words of their prayers.

> For this reason anyone who speaks in a tongue should pray that he may interpret what he says. For if I pray in a tongue, my spirit prays, but my mind is unfruitful. So what shall I do? I will pray with my spirit, but I will also pray with my mind; I will sing with my spirit, but I will also sing with my mind. If you are praising God with your spirit, how can one who finds himself among those who do not understand say "Amen" to your thanksgiving, since he does not know what you are saying? You may be giving thanks well enough, but the other man is not edified.
>
> I thank God that I speak in tongues more than all of you. But in the church I would rather speak five intelligible words to instruct others than ten thousand words in a tongue. (14:13-19)

When you pray, ask yourself, "What am I attempting to accomplish when I pray?" Your answer should be twofold: You want to speak to God on behalf of the congregation, and you want to build up your brothers and sisters through the content of what you pray.

What is true for prayer is true as well for singing. We are to teach and admonish one another through what we sing. In other words, we are to sing words that explain doctrine and encourage godly behavior. Indeed, when we sing, we should do so to build up others. That means that our song choices should be dictated primarily by the doctrinal and instructional content of the song.

We Speak to the Mind to Strengthen Faith and Change Lives

Why is it so important that everything in the time of corporate worship be spoken to the believer's mind, so that he can carefully think about what is being said? The foundation of any relationship is faith, not emotions. In our relationship with God, faith is the first step and the step that must continually undergird all that we do and are with Him. The faith that we need steps out and believes based on what we know about God, what He has said about His character, what He has said He has done in the past, what He has promised that He will do in the future and what He has said about His relationship with us.

Before we can step out in faith, we must know something about God. Until we know what God is like and what He has promised, we cannot step out in faith. That's why Paul commanded us to teach and admonish one another with all wisdom in our songs and hymns. We teach one another because we need information about God in order to know how we can trust Him. We admonish (speak to each other to encourage godly behavior) because each one of us needs to take the step that translates our hope into true, biblical faith.

When pastors or worship leaders choose songs for corporate worship, the first question they should ask is, "What am I praying God will do in the lives of the congregation through this song?" Although the question is easy to ask, it is challenging to give an informed answer for many hymns and most choruses. Answers such as "give encouragement" are not sufficient. What does the song encourage the congregation to do? What does the chorus teach that will speak to the minds of the people singing? What will they understand about God and His promises that they might have otherwise forgotten or missed? What truth will enlighten their understanding so that they can face life with renewed strength?

Fred and Janice assumed that older songs and hymns are always better than choruses. Often, however, that is just not true. They loved singing many old-time gospel songs. Yet those were little more than testimonies about how happy they were now that Jesus had come into their lives. Some old-time songs have some instruction in them, but many of them are formula choruses and songs that make the singers feel good without teaching them about God, His promises or His ways.

Some hymns do not really instruct either, even though they may be quite beautiful or stirring. Songs that repeat over and over again that we should praise God are really trite in their content. They do not explain *why* we should praise Him. What is it about God that we should praise, and why is that important? What is it about what God has done or is doing that we should praise, and why is that important? Until we speak to the mind with our songs, we are not edifying one another. We are simply stirring one another's emotions.

Again, let's remind ourselves what Paul said about speaking in tongues. It may stir us and bring a spirit of excitement and anticipation into the congregation. "But in the church I would rather speak five intelligible words to instruct others than ten thousand words in a tongue" (1 Corinthians 14:19). The same principle must apply to music. Even though a song may excite the congregation, even though a song may stir the congregation, even though a song may create a swell of anticipation among the congregation, five intelligible words that instruct the mind are better than ten thousand wonderful songs of praise. The entire worship service needs to be rethought according to what Paul taught in First Corinthians 14.

Furthermore, we cannot answer the question, "Why are we singing this particular song?" with the pat answer, "To glorify God." This is simply unacceptable. I have heard that answer so many times as an excuse for putting things that have no Christian message whatsoever into the worship service. I have many times heard secular or classical instrumental pieces performed in church services. When I have questioned such a practice, the answer I have received is, "This is something that glorifies God; therefore, it is a good thing." While everything we do must glorify God (see Colossians 3:17), including the music we write and play, we are not to assume that God wants us to put everything that glorifies Him into a worship service. We are to use music in order to edify those who are in the body of Christ, to build up others. Of course, our songs may speak about God in all of His glory, but they must do so in a manner that builds up those who are listening. The words of the song must teach and admonish the listeners. Unless the song is imparting solid information and exhortation, it is wasted.

God Requires Many People to Be a Part of Worship

One last point needs to be made here about Paul's theology concerning the worship service. Paul originally intended the gathering time of believers to involve many members of the congregation and not just pastors and worship leaders. Yet both morning and evening worship services in Western culture have been remarkably passive for the past four or five centuries in almost every tradition outside of the Quakers and Brethren. This is a travesty. Few people have a chance to contribute any real ministry during worship because only the ministers are involved.

Paul's approach is dramatically different.

> What then shall we say, brothers? When you come together, everyone has a hymn, or a word of instruction, a revelation, a tongue or an interpretation. All of these must be done for the strengthening of the church. If anyone speaks in a tongue, two—or at the most three—should speak, one at a time, and someone must interpret. If there is no interpreter, the speaker should keep quiet in the church and speak to himself and God.
>
> Two or three prophets should speak, and the others should weigh carefully what is said. And if a revelation comes to someone who is sitting down, the first speaker should stop. (1 Corinthians 14:26-30)

The apostle's order of the church service is very loose, because the congregation participates in what happens.

Some people bring songs or hymns; some people share a revelation, a tongue (interpreted) or an interpretation. Paul's approach is not carefully orchestrated, because he did not see any value in creating a "worship experience." For Paul, Christians come to worship in order to edify one another. Because this "one another" ministry does not happen in most churches today, the entire worship service is impoverished.

God desires many members of the congregation to be involved in building up the body. The whole idea of the body of Christ suggests that no one member should dominate the ministry of the Spirit. "Instead, speaking the truth in love, we will in all things grow up into him who is the Head, that is, Christ. From him the whole body, joined and held together by every supporting ligament, grows and builds itself up in love, as each part does its work" (Ephesians 4:15-16). In order for worship to be balanced, the congregation must participate, not just in responsive readings or by taking notes, but by bringing songs, revelations or interpretations. If this does not happen, the congregation will not grow, for *the whole body* is "joined and held together by every supporting ligament," not just the paid staff.

Our little congregation was looking for property to build a meeting place (we had been meeting in a high school for several years). Every property we examined was too expensive or in the wrong location, and I, the pastor, was very discouraged. One Sunday after church, we met together to discuss our frustrations. Almeda, a godly older woman in the congregation, stood up and said, "I think God is telling this church that it's time we stop looking and let Him bring the right property to us."

Almeda's comment clearly spoke to all of us. We carefully weighed what she had suggested and agreed to
spend the next few months in prayer and waiting. Within
a few weeks, a real estate agent contacted us about a
building. Before too long, we agreed on the price and
ended up converting a sausage-processing factory into a
lovely church building!

I believe that God spoke to us through Almeda. She
didn't have to say, "Thus says the Lord" for God to reveal His will to us. The congregation had to sift through
what she said (1 Corinthians 14:29) to be sure that it
was God's leading. Wayne Grudem, in his book *The
Gift of Prophecy in the New Testament and Today*, argues
that this is exactly what Paul meant when he wrote that
some people need to bring a revelation to the Church.

According to Paul, such ministries should happen during the main time we get together. "What then shall we
say, brothers? *When you come together*, everyone has a
hymn, or a word of instruction, a revelation, a tongue or
an interpretation. All of these must be done for the
strengthening of the church" (14:26). Far too often, a
chosen few dictate how the congregation meets together,
what songs they sing, the message that is preached and
what is shared. The church service becomes a passive experience. Although there are other times when people
can actively share in public ministry, Paul said it should
happen "when you come together"—and that sounds like
our Sunday morning service.

Sadly, few people in the congregation have any opportunity to contribute to the worship service. The only time the
majority of people are able to minister is by singing or giving a testimony. Many people come to church and return
home without ministering to anyone else in the entire con-

gregation. For them, worship services are like watching a television program. They sit down and relax while a few talented people do all of the work. This certainly is not Paul's understanding of our purpose in coming together.

Those who worship in the shadow of the cross care less about how much they enjoy worship and much more about how God is teaching others to know Him and love others. They deny their own desires and seek the best interests of their brothers and sisters. While others at first might object that Christians ought to come to church to "worship God," those who worship in the shadow of the cross know better: We worship God through our sacrificial ministries to others. If we come to church to serve, then our service to our brothers and sisters becomes our offering of worship to our exalted Savior.

This approach makes sense of everything we have already learned about worship in the New Testament. True offerings of worship center on giving up our rights for the sake of others, of living out the life and death of Jesus Christ in our service to the lost and the saved.

QUESTION:
How does God want Christians to worship together?

PRINCIPLE 14:

Everything we do in corporate worship should build up fellow believers. We should sing and speak truth to their minds so that they will grow in their understanding of God and learn to live in godliness.

---

*   *   *

Worship service, Sunday morning, June 3

The Spirit of God did not descend in shining flashes of glory upon the worship service at First Community Church. There were no blasts of revelation, no shouts of exultation. The service was what it would have been for any other congregation, a fairly normal time of worship.

Of course, because it was the first Sunday in more than three months that music was included, it seemed that every song, Scripture reading and testimony had more life to it. There was no question about it—music dramatically deepened the intensity of their time together.

Even so, the real blessing of the service came when there was no music. Charles and Fred stood before the congregation and both asked forgiveness for what they had done over the past year. The whole congregation was silent. Even those choir members who knew much of the story felt uneasy as they spoke. It was a difficult thing to do, especially for Fred. For a while after they shared, no one moved, no one spoke. Pastor Jeff let the silence linger within the congregation. After a long while, he quietly suggested a time of open prayer. At first, the silence continued to hang over the pews. Then Jeff heard a soft voice earnestly praying from the front row. It was Hazel. "Lord," she prayed, "search my heart. Try me and know my thoughts. Please let me have Fred's courage to examine my own heart and make sure that I have nothing against my brother or sister." Soon another voice echoed Hazel's request. Before the service finished, several men and women had opened their hearts before God in humble confession.

Something very meaningful happened during that service. Perhaps it was the prayer the night before, perhaps the specific mix of choruses and hymns, perhaps the heightened awareness coming from having music back in the service. Most likely, however, it was the honest confessions of weakness and pain before brothers and sisters in worship. That morning, people left First Community Church convinced that they had learned from God.

The sad thing was that Rick and Jeri were not there. Fred's confession had gone far, but only the Lord could finish the job. Worship wars are like that. They leave wounded in their wake. Even worse, not all of the wounded find healing over time. If there was anything to learn from the whole sordid affair, it was this: Christians cannot afford to demand their own way in the midst of a worship war. The price others pay for our sins is just too costly.

Note

1. Johannes P. Louw and Eugene A. Nida, editors, *Greek English Lexicon of the New Testament, Based on Semantic Domains, Second Edition* (New York: United Bible Societies, 1988, 1989), p. 415.

THIRTEEN

What Can I Learn about Worship from the Book of Revelation?

QUESTION:
What can I learn about worship
from the book of Revelation?

PRINCIPLE 15:

Worship must include constant reminders that
Christ is returning, that He will make all wrongs
right and that all those who know Him will be transformed at His coming.

The rumbling stops. A stillness floods the air and brilliance engulfs the twilight.

A trumpet sounds.

You look up. He is there, the sky unrolling before Him in welcome worship.

Lights explode inside your mind's eye. Life roars through your veins.

And all of a sudden you know everything that before you had only guessed.

Angelic voices you have always recognized, though you've never heard them before, burst into song above you, around you, under you.

Your universe erupts into color.

Your senses surge.

Your muscles energize.

You are alive. For the first time, you are really alive.

You look up again. Now you see Him as He really is.

And He looks at you, right at you, and smiles. *Come up here, My child,* His eyes say. Freedom has begun.

All in an instant, in the twinkling of an eye.

Now your song joins the voices you hear. Following your song, you rise, bursting with joy that pours out in soaring cascades, riding the waves of a hundred million cries of joy. Free at last. Free at last.

All in an instant, in the twinkling of an eye.

When We See Him Face-to-Face

We cannot truly comprehend what worship will be like in the new heaven and new earth. In the future, we will be so different in our minds and emotions that whatever we understand now is only a distant echo of reality. The book of Revelation cracks the window open wide enough for us to catch a glimpse of worship in the new heaven and new earth, but only a glimpse. For the best part, we will just have to wait until we hear the trumpet sound.

Revelation 7:9-10 says,

> After this I looked and there before me was a great multitude that no one could count, from every nation, tribe, people and language, standing before the throne and in front of the Lamb. They were wearing white robes and were holding palm branches in their hands. And they cried out in a loud voice:
> "Salvation belongs to our God,
> who sits on the throne,
> and to the Lamb."

No one knows for certain who these martyrs are. Are they souls without resurrected bodies, as those "under the altar" may be in Revelation 6:9-11? Are they the martyrs who were killed during the Great Tribulation, or are they all those who have died in Christ? Do they have resurrected bodies?

I am going to treat them as if they are all of God's people from Adam through the last believer to be saved. I believe that they are standing before God in glorious resurrected bodies. What does John tell us about these resurrected human beings?

We will stand before the throne.

> At once I was in the Spirit, and there before me was a throne in heaven with someone sitting on it. And the one who sat there had the appearance of jasper and carnelian. A rainbow, resembling an emerald, encircled the throne. Surrounding the throne were twenty-four other thrones, and seated on them were

twenty-four elders. They were dressed in white and had crowns of gold on their heads. From the throne came flashes of lightning, rumblings and peals of thunder. Before the throne, seven lamps were blazing. These are the seven spirits of God. Also before the throne there was what looked like a sea of glass, clear as crystal.

In the center, around the throne, were four living creatures, and they were covered with eyes, in front and in back. The first living creature was like a lion, the second was like an ox, the third had a face like a man, the fourth was like a flying eagle. Each of the four living creatures had six wings and was covered with eyes all around, even under his wings. Day and night they never stop saying:

"Holy, holy, holy
is the Lord God Almighty,
who was, and is, and is to come." (Revelation 4:2-8)

The multitude, which I take to be all the resurrected saints of all ages, will stand before this throne. The rainbow, thrones, flashes of lightning, peals of thunder, lamps of fire, living creatures and elders will surround them, but they will not fear. Their resurrected eyes will only delight, because God will have recreated their eyes to see such sights as these. The thoughts of such bizarre experiences may turn off Christians from thinking about their future glory in heaven. They subconsciously assume that such alien ordeals will be disagreeable at best. This would be true for now, because power like this would simply overload our human eyes. In the future, however, God will reequip our eyes (1 John 3:1-3).

Our resurrected eyes will see God and the Lamb as they really are. We will look upon them in all of their wonder. "Dear friends, now we are children of God, and what we will be has not yet been made known. But we know that when he appears, we shall be like him, for we shall see him as he is" (1 John 3:2). We shall see Christ just as He is! Until this point, when human eyes beheld the living Son of God, they saw only what flesh could see. The apostles' eyes saw a Miracle Worker, a Teacher, a Messiah, a King. Our present eyes can see only flesh, but our future eyes will go beyond the flesh to see the Son of God as He is. "No eye has seen, no ear has heard, no mind has conceived what God has prepared for those who love him" (1 Corinthians 2:9). Someday we will see Jesus as He really is, in all of His glory and wonder.

We will be before Him. On that future day, we will all sing with joy when we encounter the true presence of God. He will be right there before us, and we will gaze at His hands, His side and His feet and understand His cross for the first time. We will see Him as Lamb, as Conqueror, as King, as Brother, as Eternal God, as Son and as Lord of Eternity, and we will understand those things. They will not overwhelm us. We will see Him just as He is.

I suspect as well that we will see the Father. Revelation 22:3-5 tells us,

> No longer will there be any curse. The throne of God and of the Lamb will be in the city, and his servants will serve him. They will see his face, and his name will be on their foreheads. There will be no more night. They will not need the light of a lamp or the light of the sun, for the Lord God will give them light. And they will reign for ever and ever.

This may mean that we will see Christ's face in the throne room, but I suspect that the word *his* here may refer to the Father, since this is the name that God will write on our foreheads.

> Him who overcomes I will make a pillar in the temple of my God. Never again will he leave it. I will write on him the name of my God and the name of the city of my God, the new Jerusalem, which is coming down out of heaven from my God; and I will also write on him my new name. (Revelation 3:12)

Paul promised the same exquisite joy. "Now we see but a poor reflection as in a mirror; then we shall see face to face. Now I know in part; then I shall know fully, even as I am fully known" (1 Corinthians 13:12).

Moses could not truly see God face-to-face. When he asked to see God's glory, the Lord revealed only His aftereffects (translated as "back," but better understood as the effects of His glory). You see, God knew that Moses could not survive a face-to-face encounter, so He told him, "You cannot see my face, for no one may see me and live" (Exodus 33:20). In the future, however, we will know Him face-to-face. We will see Him and live. We will hear His true voice and not fear ever again.

We will be clothed in white robes. The linen will be the righteous acts of the saints, but we have done nothing that is truly righteous. "All of us have become like one who is unclean, and all our righteous acts are like filthy rags; we all shrivel up like a leaf, and like the wind our sins sweep us away" (Isaiah 64:6). Our righteous acts are filthy when compared with Christ's true righteousness. So God performs the wonder of all eternity: He cleanses the filthiness of our robes with Christ's blood. The saints "have washed their robes and made them white in the blood of the Lamb" (Revelation 7:14). We will never feel shame again. We will rejoice in what God has done for us in Christ. And we will have the joy of knowing that the best we ever did for Christ and His people on earth was nothing until Christ cleansed it with His blood.

We will carry palm branches.

We will praise Him.

We will serve Him. Latreuo is the word used to describe religious service to God. The writer of Hebrews used *latreuo* when portraying the priests' work in offering sacrifices (Hebrews 9:9; 10:1-2; 13:10). We have seen already that Paul and the Hebrews writer also used the word to describe the Christian's religious service to God, which is our sacrificial ministry to others for Christ's sake. In the future, we will serve God in a new way, different from the Hebrew priests, who offered sacrifices, and different from Christians in this age, who offer themselves.

We shall offer this service continually (Revelation 7:15) as God's bond servants (22:3). What will that religious service be? The text does not give a clue. Most Christians assume that this "temple service" to God will be our praise to Him, but the text does not suggest that. We must be careful not to assume what we cannot even guess. After all, what Old Testament saint would have guessed that our present-age offerings would be our lives in service for others? In the same way, our future religious service to the Father remains a mystery.

We will never suffer again.

The Lamb will be our Shepherd.

This tells me that we will always have a relationship with Jesus, even when we stand before Him face-to-face. One of the greatest lies we can believe about eternity is that we will just stand before the throne and praise God forever and ever. This is simply untrue. We will be profoundly involved in very meaningful work. After all, the Scriptures tell us that we will reign with Him. We will rule on the earth, apparently in the millennium. "You have made them to be a kingdom and priests to serve our God, and they will reign on the earth" (5:10). "They will be priests of God and of Christ and will reign with him for a thousand years" (20:6). In addition, we will be judging angels (1 Corinthians 6:3). Even after the millennium, when God has destroyed the earth and created a new heaven and a new earth, we will continue to reign with Him. "There will be no more night. They will not need the light of a lamp or the light of the sun, for the Lord God will give them light. And they will reign for ever and ever" (Revelation 22:5).

Remember, the greatest commandment is to "love the LORD your God with all your heart and with all your soul and with all your strength" (Deuteronomy 6:5). God created us to love Him and one another. That will never change. He will continue to walk with us in love. The Lord Jesus will continue to shepherd us as we reign *with* Him. He will continue to lead us to drink of the living waters. We will continue to know Him in a personal way. We will continue to know God as our Father, but now face-to-face, no longer in a mystery.

We will sing to God. On that future day we will sing the song Moses sang on the shores of the Red Sea. After God had guided Israel to safety through the sea, Moses led the people in a glorious song of victory. So we will sing of God's victory over our enemies of sin, death and Satan. We will also sing to the Lamb, whose works will be great and marvelous on the day when He defeats all the nations.

> And I saw what looked like a sea of glass mixed with fire and, standing beside the sea, those who had been

victorious over the beast and his image and over the
number of his name. They held harps given them by
God and sang the song of Moses the servant of God
and the song of the Lamb:

"Great and marvelous are your deeds,
    Lord God Almighty.
Just and true are your ways,
    King of the ages.
Who will not fear you, O Lord,
    and bring glory to your name?
For you alone are holy.
All nations will come
    and worship before you,
for your righteous acts have been
        revealed." (Revelation 15:2-4)

Notice the words of the song. Even in heaven we will
praise God with meaningful words, rather than simply
crying out with emotional exultation. God's works are
great, His ways are true, and everyone will fear Him because He has made known to us His righteous acts.

We will be His bride. The Bible portrays the bride as
gloriously beautiful. John's description of the scene
dazzles the heart.

One of the seven angels who had the seven bowls
full of the seven last plagues came and said to me,
"Come, I will show you the bride, the wife of the
Lamb." And he carried me away in the Spirit to a
mountain great and high, and showed me the Holy
City, Jerusalem, coming down out of heaven from
God. It shone with the glory of God, and its brilliance was like that of a very precious jewel, like a jas-
per, clear as crystal. (Revelation 21:9-11)

We will be glorious when we worship our Groom, our Husband. Jesus died to clothe us in magnificent wedding raiment.

> Husbands, love your wives, just as Christ loved the church and gave himself up for her to make her holy, cleansing her by the washing with water through the word, and to present her to himself as a radiant church, without stain or wrinkle or any other blemish, but holy and blameless. (Ephesians 5:25-27)

The New Testament delights in describing our future state as glorious, because this has always been God's plan.

When we praise Him, we will shine. Our glory will be the joy of the entire universe. "The creation waits in eager expectation for the sons of God to be revealed" (Romans 8:19). God called us to make us glorious. Through our earthen vessels, He already is transforming us to produce His glory. "And we, who with unveiled faces all reflect the Lord's glory, are being transformed into his likeness with ever-increasing glory, which comes from the Lord, who is the Spirit" (2 Corinthians 3:18). Today, our glory is in the cross. In the future, we will shine with glory in our very beings.

Does Revelation Offer a Pattern for Today's Worship?

Many writers and pastors use the book of Revelation to describe worship here on earth, but they may be approaching the subject in an incorrect way. First, humans do little worship in Revelation. There are many songs in Revelation, but surprisingly, Revelation 15:2-4 alone depicts the saints singing. Elsewhere heavenly elders, creatures and angels perform singing. Likewise, Revelation

never pictures the saints bowing before the throne, although many other mighty creatures regularly fall down.
(Note: Two times in Revelation a messenger rebuked
John for worshiping him and told him to worship God
alone.) One assumes that we will bow before God's
throne, but the text does not say.

I am not convinced that Revelation says we will
mimic angelic worship. Angels have a dramatically different relationship with God. They are servants on our
behalf (Hebrews 1:14), but they are not God's adopted
sons and daughters. We will worship God based upon
our relationship with Him as His children. I suspect our
worship may follow a different path than that of angels.

Second, worship here and now has to differ from worship in eternity because our roles now are different than
what they will be. Right now we are the temple of the
Holy Spirit. We are the priesthood and the sacrifice of
praise. Our lives are offerings to God. His glory shines
through our weakness. But this will change in the new
heaven and the new earth. God and the Lamb will be the
temple. Christ the Lamb will be the sacrifice.

> I did not see a temple in the city, because the Lord
> God Almighty and the Lamb are its temple. The city
> does not need the sun or the moon to shine on it, for
> the glory of God gives it light, and the Lamb is its
> lamp. (Revelation 21:22-23)

Therefore, we should not attempt to model our present
worship on that future worship, any more than we
should attempt to model our present worship on past
worship (temples, sacrifices, etc.). We do not know how
we are going to offer religious service to God in the fu-

ture, but it *has* to be different from what we are doing now.

Everywhere we go, His presence will bathe us, because God and the Lamb will be the light of the universe. What does that mean for worship? No longer will anything separate us from the actual presence of God. No longer will we wonder what God is thinking and doing. No longer will the veil of flesh cloak God's nearness. We will not merely see the presence of God, but it will wash over us, envelop us, energize us, talk to us and, most of all, fellowship with us. His presence will not be a mindless power that controls us, but a loving Shepherd who guides us and a gracious Father who embraces us with love.

We will see Jesus in all of His glory, but if the book of Revelation is any indication, we will especially see Him forever as the Lamb who was slain. Revelation describes Jesus Christ twenty-eight times as the Lamb. Three of those times we see Jesus specifically as the Lamb who was slain. "Then I saw a Lamb, looking as if it had been slain, standing in the center of the throne, encircled by the four living creatures and the elders. He had seven horns and seven eyes, which are the seven spirits of God sent out into all the earth" (Revelation 5:6; see also Revelation 5:12 and 13:8). Even in the glories of heaven, the cross stands glorious. Of course, how could we ever cease to praise Him and love Him for His cross when even our clothing is pure only through the blood of the Lamb?

How Reading Revelation Should Impact Our Worship

Sometimes I wonder if Christians in America really get excited about the promise that Jesus is coming back. We do not seem to sing about it very often, judging by the fact that almost all the songs about the Second Coming are very old. Some pundits say that Americans are most concerned about here and now, and that may be true. Yet the writers of the New Testament were seemingly obsessed by their longing for Christ's return. Perhaps a renewed study of the book of Revelation could help us revitalize our excitement about God's promises for our coming eternal glory. If we want to see the Church wake up in these last days, we need to consider carefully these three foundational principles out of Revelation.

We must put Christ's return back into the center of our worship. We have several hints in the New Testament that Christ's return stood at the center of Christian worship in that era. Many scholars believe that Paul quoted a beautiful Christian hymn in Philippians 2:6-11. That hymn not only describes Christ's humiliation, but also the day when every human being will confess Him as Lord of the universe.

> Therefore God exalted him to the highest place
> and gave him the name that is above every name,
> that at the name of Jesus every knee should bow,
> in heaven and on earth and under the earth,
> and every tongue confess that Jesus Christ is Lord,
> to the glory of God the Father. (Philippians 2:9-11)

This will not happen until Jesus returns in glory.

A second example shows us that when Christians partook of the Lord's Supper, they were proclaiming the Lord's death "until he comes" (1 Corinthians 11:26). One more example may be a hymn or simply a Christian proverb. "Here is a trustworthy saying: If we died with him, we will also live with him; if we endure, we will also reign with him. If we disown him, he will also disown us; if we are faithless, he will remain faithful, for he cannot disown himself" (2 Timothy 2:11-13). The New Testament gives us few examples of songs, and the few we do have mention our future hope. We can surmise that our future resurrection glory should return to a place of prominence in our worship times today.

We must emphasize Christ's return to help our congregation face persecution and distress. Revelation reminds us that God is in control of all history. Even though much of the book gives us a clear picture of the future, that is not its greatest value. Revelation teaches us how to suffer under persecution. In this letter, Jesus constantly commands us to overcome, to persevere, to stand our ground. "He who overcomes will inherit all this, and I will be his God and he will be my son" (Revelation 21:7). When we read Revelation, we know for certain that Jesus Christ has already won the battle. No one can ultimately defeat us. Satan will persecute the saints, but he cannot defeat those who have been washed in the blood of Christ. "They overcame him by the blood of the Lamb and by the word of their testimony; they did not love their lives so much as to shrink from death" (12:11). Death itself has no power over God's sons and daughters. "Blessed and holy are those who have part in the first resurrection. The second death has no power over them, but they will be priests of God and of Christ and will reign with him for a thousand years" (20:6). Keeping those truths in front of us enables us to withstand the storms of life. What a wonderful encouragement we bring to our congregation when we think on these truths during our time of corporate worship! Whether through song, spoken word, drama or testimony, these truths can strengthen the weak and enable them to stand strong.

Our present lives are nothing compared with our future glory. A friend of mine struggled about buying a new house. Most of his Christian friends could not understand the nature of his struggle. For them, buying a house promised equity, a nest egg for the future. Buying a house brought security and provided stability. My friend, however, kept thinking about what Jesus taught regarding equity, security and stability. Houses cannot really offer any of those. Moths destroy, thieves break in and steal, and rust eats away our "investments" in this world (Matthew 6:19). In a passage that ends up discussing His second coming, Jesus said, "Sell your possessions and give to the poor. Provide purses for yourselves that will not wear out, a treasure in heaven that will not be exhausted, where no thief comes near and no moth destroys. For where your treasure is, there your heart will be also" (Luke 12:33-34). Revelation teaches us that we should never invest in this world, for it is passing away. If for no other reason than this, Christians should read from the book of Revelation every week, that they might redirect their energies toward eternity.

Revelation promises us that one day we will know God and Jesus face-to-face. That relationship defines worship in the new heaven and new earth. That relationship transforms worship from action to the fulfillment of our deepest hopes and dreams. Worship will not simply be singing and praise, although certainly just as God will sing over us (Zephaniah 3:17), we will sing over Him. Worship will be what happens when the infinite God of the universe recreates His beloved children so that they can enjoy Him and love Him and know His love and walk in His love for all eternity. In light of our future, we should continually put Christ's return at the center of our times of corporate worship.

Of the top twenty-five choruses sung in America according to Christian Copyright Licensing International in August 2001, not one mentioned the return of Jesus Christ. Surely even among many churches that sing only hymns, we would find the same pattern. How impoverished our worship has become!

QUESTION:
What can I learn about worship
from the book of Revelation?

PRINCIPLE 15:

Worship must include constant reminders that Christ is returning, that He will make all wrongs right and that all those who know Him will be transformed at His coming.

EPILOGUE:

If You Find Yourself
in a Worship War . . .

You may know stories very similar to the fictional one I have told on these pages. Worshipers like Charles and Fred often struggle terribly. They attend churches with worship styles foreign to their own preferences and often become bitter. How should they deal with such frustration?

First, Christians need to redefine worship the way the New Testament does. Our real worship does not happen during the singing time on Sunday morning. I know someone who recently attended a church service that was outside of his comfort zone. It started off to be a very unpleasant experience. Then he realized that his worship would be in how he loved the people who were there. He began to pray that God would minister to them through the songs that were being sung, and that God would help them grow through the time they were spending in the service. My friend found that by loving his brothers and sisters, he was worshiping God.

Second, we should recognize that when our brothers and sisters are praising God in ways that offend us, God may not see them in that way. Their way of praising Him may be very pleasing in His sight. Paul reminded us that God looks at the heart, not at the particular way of expression:

> Who are you to judge someone else's servant? To his own master he stands or falls. And he will stand, for the Lord is able to make him stand.

One man considers one day more sacred than another; another man considers every day alike. Each one should be fully convinced in his own mind. He who regards one day as special, does so to the Lord. He who eats meat, eats to the Lord, for he gives thanks to God; and he who abstains, does so to the Lord and gives thanks to God. For none of us lives to himself alone and none of us dies to himself alone. If we live, we live to the Lord; and if we die, we die to the Lord. So, whether we live or die, we belong to the Lord. (Romans 14:4-8)

Third, when you are a part of a service where activities are going on that are not edifying, pray that God would forgive those who are doing this and that He will accept their worship. When Judah celebrated a long-overdue Passover, many of those who joined in were not ritually pure. Hezekiah knew that nothing could be done about it at that point.

But Hezekiah prayed for them, saying, "May the LORD, who is good, pardon everyone who sets his heart on seeking God—the LORD, the God of his fathers—even if he is not clean according to the rules of the sanctuary." And the LORD heard Hezekiah and healed the people. (2 Chronicles 30:18-20)

Rather than condemn the people, pray that God would receive their worship.

Fourth, live a life of sacrificial love before the people of the congregation. Show the cross of Christ by your lifestyle. When you live the cross, your testimony about true worship becomes believable. Paul often exhorted his readers to follow his example. Do the same and you will see much fruit.

Fifth, pray for an opportunity to speak to those who are leading the corporate worship service. That should be your last option, after months and months of prayer and seeking God. Do not argue with them, but explain to them what the Scriptures teach about worship. Let God do His work, which means that you must not cause division in the body.

While writing this book, time and time again I encountered those who had been hurt by worship wars in churches across the country. How ironic that our greatest service of worship is to present our lives for the *sake of others*. How seldom that happens when we fight and bicker among ourselves over the proper worship style. We must go back to the basics in worship, which is the cross of Jesus Christ. Only when we worship in the shadow of the cross is our worship meaningful.

God Will Judge Our Worship by Our Lives

At the end of a day, we sometimes look back over what has happened and decide whether it has been a good or bad day. God has told us that He will judge our days, but He will use a different ruler to measure whether they have been good or not.

God will not judge how we have felt about Jesus but how we have walked with Him. The real test will not be whether we have enjoyed Jesus but whether we have loved Him. Love always stands as the only true measure of any real relationship.

Love is not a feeling but an attitude. Treasuring the other person, love always chooses whatever is truly best for him. Sacrifice loses its pain when compared to the needs of the other person. Love goes all the way to the cross if that will bring life to another.

To love Jesus is to listen to Him and obey Him. "If you love me, you will obey what I command" (John 14:15). We will treasure what He says and apply it to our lives. "Therefore everyone who hears these words of mine and puts them into practice is like a wise man who built his house on the rock" (Matthew 7:24).

Loving Jesus will cause us to invest in heaven, where He reigns. "But store up for yourselves treasures in heaven, where moth and rust do not destroy, and where thieves do not break in and steal. For where your treasure is, there your heart will be also" (6:20-21).

Loving Jesus will lead us to care for those whom He loves.

> Then the King will say to those on his right, "Come, you who are blessed by my Father; take your inheritance, the kingdom prepared for you since the creation of the world. For I was hungry and you gave me something to eat, I was thirsty and you gave me something to drink, I was a stranger and you invited me in, I needed clothes and you clothed me, I was sick and you looked after me, I was in prison and you came to visit me." (25:34-36)

Loving Jesus will drive us to fulfill the task He has entrusted to us.

> The man who had received the five talents brought the other five. "Master," he said, "you entrusted me with five talents. See, I have gained five more."
> His master replied, "Well done, good and faithful

servant! You have been faithful with a few things; I will put you in charge of many things. Come and share you master's happiness!" (Matthew 25:20-21)

The race will be hard, but those who love Him will run it to the end. "I have fought the good fight, I have finished the race, I have kept the faith. Now there is in store for me the crown of righteousness, which the Lord, the righteous Judge, will award to me on that day—and not only to me, but also to all who have longed for his appearing" (2 Timothy 4:7-8).

At the end of the day, God will not judge our lives by our worship, but our worship by our lives. If we felt His presence, saw His miracles and experienced visions and wonders, would that make our day a good one? No. Jesus said that many will come to Him with all of that and yet not enter into His joy (Matthew 7:22-23). He will not measure our love by what we felt, but by how much we made Him our treasure. As much as we invested our lives in Him, that is how much we treasured Him.

And if we love Him, we will love His cross.

Look upon Him there as He suffered and see the kind of love He had for those who cursed Him. Go out and do the same for others. Then come back and stand again before that same cross. Suddenly, you see the thorns in His brow and hear Him gasp, "Father, forgive them, for they do not know what they are doing" (Luke 23:34). Return to your persecutors and utter those same words as they slander you and turn against you. Then bow again on Golgotha and see the nails in His feet. Every time you carry His cross and then return to stand before Him, you will understand more of His love. Bearing His cross teaches you to adore His love. We can understand Jesus' love only as we practice it toward others. Worship Him by imitating Him, dying with Him and then adoring Him.

We will worship the way it was meant to be.

The world does not need anger—it has seen enough. The world does not need protest—it has heard enough. And condemnation? It is already condemned (John 3:18). The world needs to see the glory of the cross, the glory of the cross in us, in our lives, in our commitment and in our deaths for it.

Principles of Biblical Worship

QUESTION:
Why should I worship God?

PRINCIPLE 1:

A: God created me so that I could know Him and love Him. Worship flows from my love relationship with God.

B: All relationships are based on trust. In my worship, I step out and trust what God has said about Himself and His ways.

C: When I sin, I am refusing to love God and therefore cannot worship Him. My sin also drives me to hide from Him.

QUESTION:
Why do I bring offerings to God in my worship?

PRINCIPLE 2:

I bring God offerings as a way to present myself to Him, asking Him to accept me as His servant.

237

QUESTION:
What makes my worship acceptable to God?

PRINCIPLE 3:

God accepts my worship only if my heart is genuine before Him.

QUESTION:
Why did the Old Testament
require animal sacrifices in worship?

PRINCIPLE 4:

Worshipers brought animal sacrifices so that God's wrath might fall on the sacrifice rather than on the sinner. The sacrifice was a picture of what God would later do to Jesus Christ, the true Lamb of God.

QUESTION:
According to Moses, what does
God require of me for worship?

PRINCIPLE 5:

A: According to Moses, God requires me to put myself in my proper relationship with Him.

QUESTION:
According to Moses, what did God
require of Israel for worship?

PRINCIPLE 5:

B: According to Moses, God required Israel to serve
Him with all of their hearts through offerings and
sacrifice.

QUESTION:
According to Moses, how did
music relate to Israel's worship?

PRINCIPLE 5:

C: God did not reveal to Moses what part music was
to play in Israel's worship.

QUESTION:
According to Moses, what else did
God require of Israel for worship?

PRINCIPLE 5:

D: According to Moses, God required Israel to worship Him by remembering His mighty saving acts.

QUESTION:
What makes my worship holy?

PRINCIPLE 6:

My worship is holy only if what I bring God is wholly
His.

QUESTION:
How can I tell if I am committing idolatry?

PRINCIPLE 7:

A: I am committing idolatry when I change God to
make Him easier to understand and approach.

B: I am committing idolatry when I seek to bypass
my relationship with God in order to gain whatever I
desire.

QUESTION:
How should I worship God in song?

PRINCIPLE 8:

A: Using the Psalms as my model, my songs should
bring to God both my sorrows and my joys.

B: Using the Psalms as my model, I should focus my
praise on who God is and what He does, rather than
on how I feel about Him.

QUESTION:
What did the prophets teach about worship?

PRINCIPLE 9:

A: The prophets exposed Israel's idolatry and revealed why the people turned away from the Lord.

B: The prophets taught that God did not criticize Israel's methods of worship. He instead criticized the fact that the people's worship was not in truth, because they did not truly love God nor did they demonstrate love for their neighbors.

C: The prophets taught that God removed His presence from the temple right before Babylon destroyed it. God's presence would not return until the Messiah came.

D: The prophets taught that when the Messiah came, both Jew and Gentile would bring acceptable sacrifices to God in restored worship.

QUESTION:
Now that Jesus has come,
how do I come to God to worship Him?

PRINCIPLE 10:

A: Jesus taught that He is the New Temple, so I must come to Jesus Himself in order to worship God.

B: Jesus taught that He is the replacement and fulfillment of all of Israel's feasts and rituals of worship. I
must come to Jesus to experience the true meaning
of Israel's religion.

QUESTION:
How do I worship in spirit and truth?

PRINCIPLE 11:

A: Only those who are born of the Spirit can worship
God in spirit and truth.

B: I can sense the Spirit's working in my worship
only through the results of what He does, for His
presence and work among believers are mysterious.

C: I worship in truth when the Holy Spirit's fruit
(love, joy, peace, patience, kindness, goodness, faithfulness, gentleness and self-control) accompanies my
worship.

QUESTION:
What forms do I use to bring my worship
to God, now that the temple,
priests and sacrifices have passed away?

PRINCIPLE 12:

A: All Christians are now priests who bring sacrifices
and offerings to God.

B: Both individual believers and believers as a whole are the temple where offerings and sacrifices are brought to God.

C: I present my life in service to others as a living sacrifice and offering to God.

Q U E S T I O N :
How can I experience God's glory in my worship?

P R I N C I P L E   1 3 :

God exposes His glory most completely when in weakness I die to myself, offering up my rights and comfort for the sake of others.

Q U E S T I O N :
How does God want Christians to worship together?

P R I N C I P L E   1 4 :

Everything we do in corporate worship should build up fellow believers. We should sing and speak truth to their minds so that they will grow in their understanding of God and learn to live in godliness.

QUESTION:
What can I learn about worship
from the book of Revelation?

PRINCIPLE 15:

Worship must include constant reminders that
Christ is returning, that He will make all wrongs
right and that all those who know Him will be transformed at His coming.